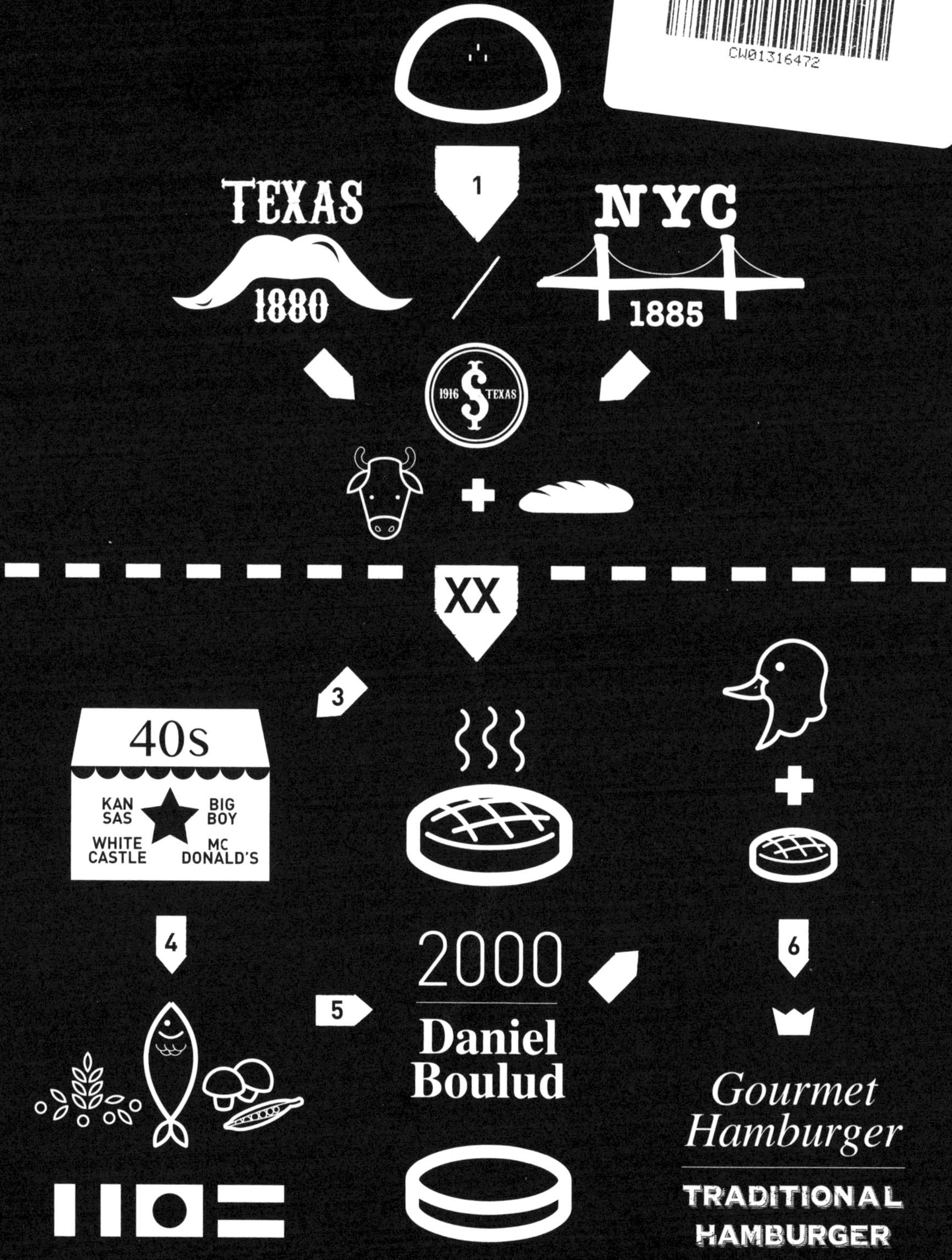

HAMBURGER GOURMET

DAVID JAPY / ÉLODIE RAMBAUD / VICTOR GARNIER

MURDOCH BOOKS

Contents

4
INTRO
GENESIS / HISTORY OF THE HAMBURGER / EQUIPMENT / TIPS

12
DISSECTION
THE HAMBURGER PIECE BY PIECE

30
PURE
100% FISH OR MEAT

90
MIX
COMBINATIONS OF MEATS AND SPICES

120
VEGGIE
100% VEGETABLE

134
AT THE CUTTING EDGE
RECIPES FROM THE CHEF

142
BLENDIES
SWEET AMERICAN TREATS WITH A FRENCH TWIST

156
ACKNOWLEDGEMENTS

158
INDEX

GENESIS

In 2010, in Santa Monica, California, I met the hamburger that was to change my life: it tasted unlike any hamburger I had ever eaten before. I realised that day that with good bread, good meat and good vegetables, the possibilities were endless.

Since then, at Blend, I've spent my time dreaming up recipes for gourmet hamburgers. We take inspiration from every cuisine, always on a quest for innovation.

The hamburger is effectively an invitation to cook and to take pleasure in eating, not to mention the sense of conviviality it inspires—people feel good around a good hamburger. It brings people together, brings them closer. What I also like is its humility: whether it contains ordinary minced beef or the latest recipe from a great chef, the hamburger stays in its place, snug and warm between two slices of bun, and can be enjoyed by everyone.

The hamburger has this distinctive feature: it is almost as much fun to make as it is to eat.

In the preparatory stage, we turned our attention to the search for the perfect blend that gives the gourmet hamburger its special quality. A blend is a mixture, a fusion of qualities. It consists of selecting different cuts of beef for their quality and advantages, and combining them to achieve an optimum balance of texture and taste.

I then happily crossed paths with Yves-Marie le Bourdonnec—a butcher in love with his trade, as passionate about meat as I can be about hamburgers. Together, thanks to his expertise and know-how, and after countless experiments, we finally found our blend.

Once this is achieved, any variation is possible.

Welcome to Blend. We wish you a great deal of pleasure making our gourmet hamburgers. Don't hesitate to make our recipes your own.

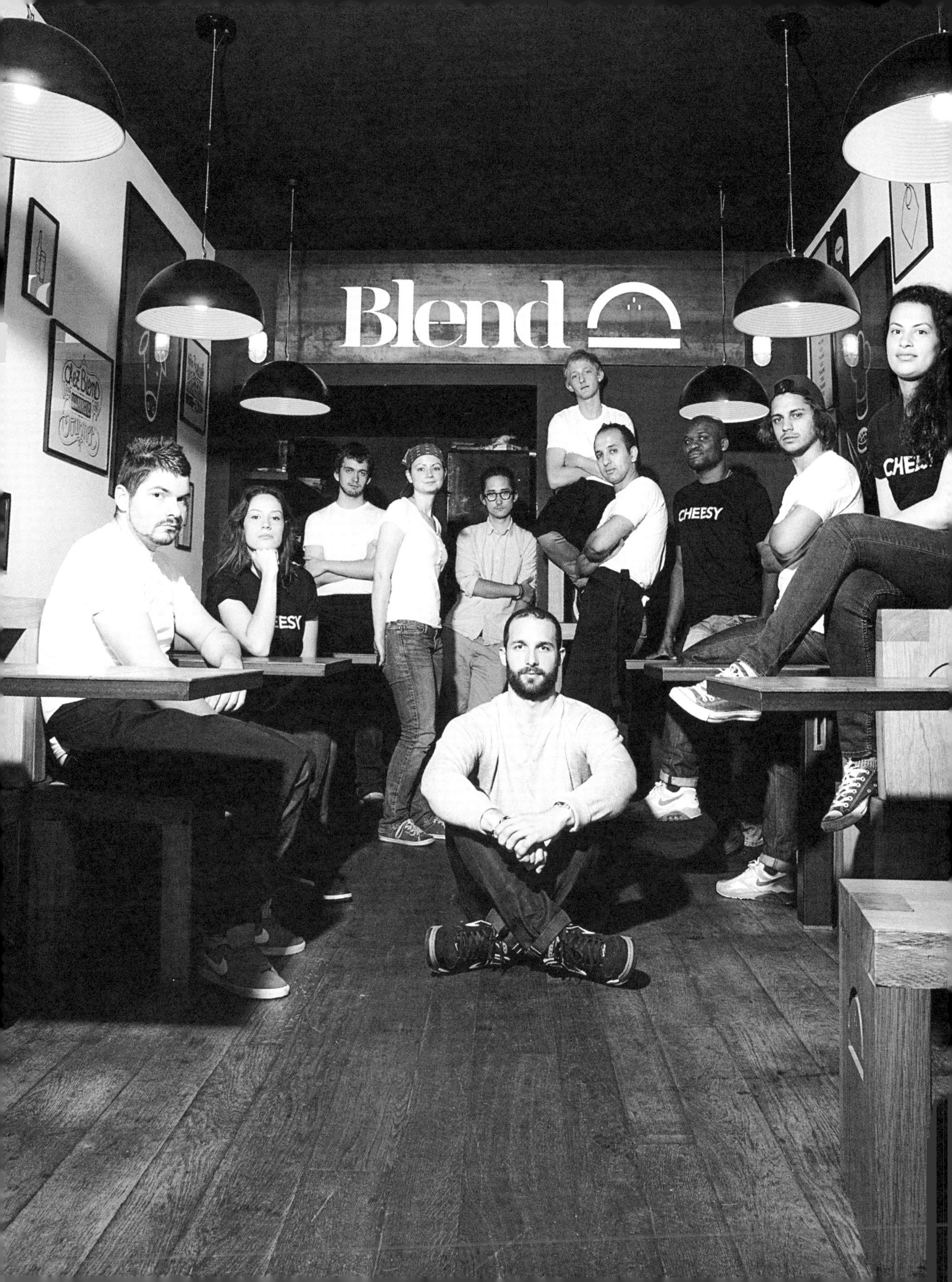
Blend
CHEESY
CHEESY
CHEESY

HISTORY OF THE HAMBURGER

While the first traces of minced meat or patties date back to the thirteenth century with the Mongols, we are only concerned here with hamburgers, namely, a sandwich into which a meat patty has been inserted.

1/ It is not said often enough, but none of this would have happened if, at the beginning of the nineteenth century, a certain Karl Drais had not invented the meat mincer. Some claim that the hamburger was born in Texas in 1880, originating with Fletcher Davis. Or else it might have been the Menches Brothers of Hamburg, New York, who allegedly invented it around 1885. The same year, in Wisconsin, a little 15-year-old genius by the name of Charlie Nagreen had the wonderful idea of putting his meatballs between two slices of bread, to increase his sales. For others, it comes from New Haven, and we owe it to Louis Lassen — in Connecticut, the restaurant Louis' Lunch still proudly displays today the information that, in 1900, the manager at the time had the brilliant idea of putting boiled beef between two slices of bread to satisfy a customer who wanted to eat on the run! Finally, in 1916, there is evidence of a certain hamburger sold by Walter Anderson in Wichita, Kansas. While historians recognise that the invention of a popular dish can't come down to a particular individual, what is certain is that the earliest forms of hamburger were slices of traditional bread and sliced or chopped meat.

2/ The minced meat patty between two slices of bread appeared at the end of the nineteenth century or beginning of the twentieth century. It was only a little later, still in the United States, when they realised the patty had to be seared at a high temperature to make it crusty and that a round bun was more convenient for eating in the hands without making a mess, that the hamburger was really born: a meat patty between the two halves of a round bun.

3/ The first hamburger chains soon saw the light of day: White Castle in Wichita, Kansas, Big Boy in Glendale, California, and then McDonald's in San Bernardino, California. We have reached about the 1940s.

4/ The rise of the hamburger was at first considerable in the United States, where every state and every city had its own speciality, its own hamburger recipe. Then, up to the 2000s, the hamburger went international. It took on influences from every cuisine and developed in complexity: teriyaki sauce, rice cake bun, fish ... Every culture makes it its own.

5/ In the early 2000s, the hamburger underwent a significant new development: chefs finally became interested in it. Daniel Boulud, a French chef based in New York, became the figurehead of this trend by putting on his restaurant menu a foie gras hamburger for $29. This new fine-dining approach went international and chefs around the world started to consider the hamburger with a great deal of attention.

6/ In California, after almost a decade, we have witnessed the birth of two new categories of hamburger. On the one hand, the chefs' hamburgers, rebaptised 'gourmet hamburgers' by the food critics. These are distinguished from traditional hamburgers by their sophisticated ingredients and refined recipes. On the other hand, purists reappropriate the fast-food hamburger by simplifying and streamlining it, using only quality ingredients.

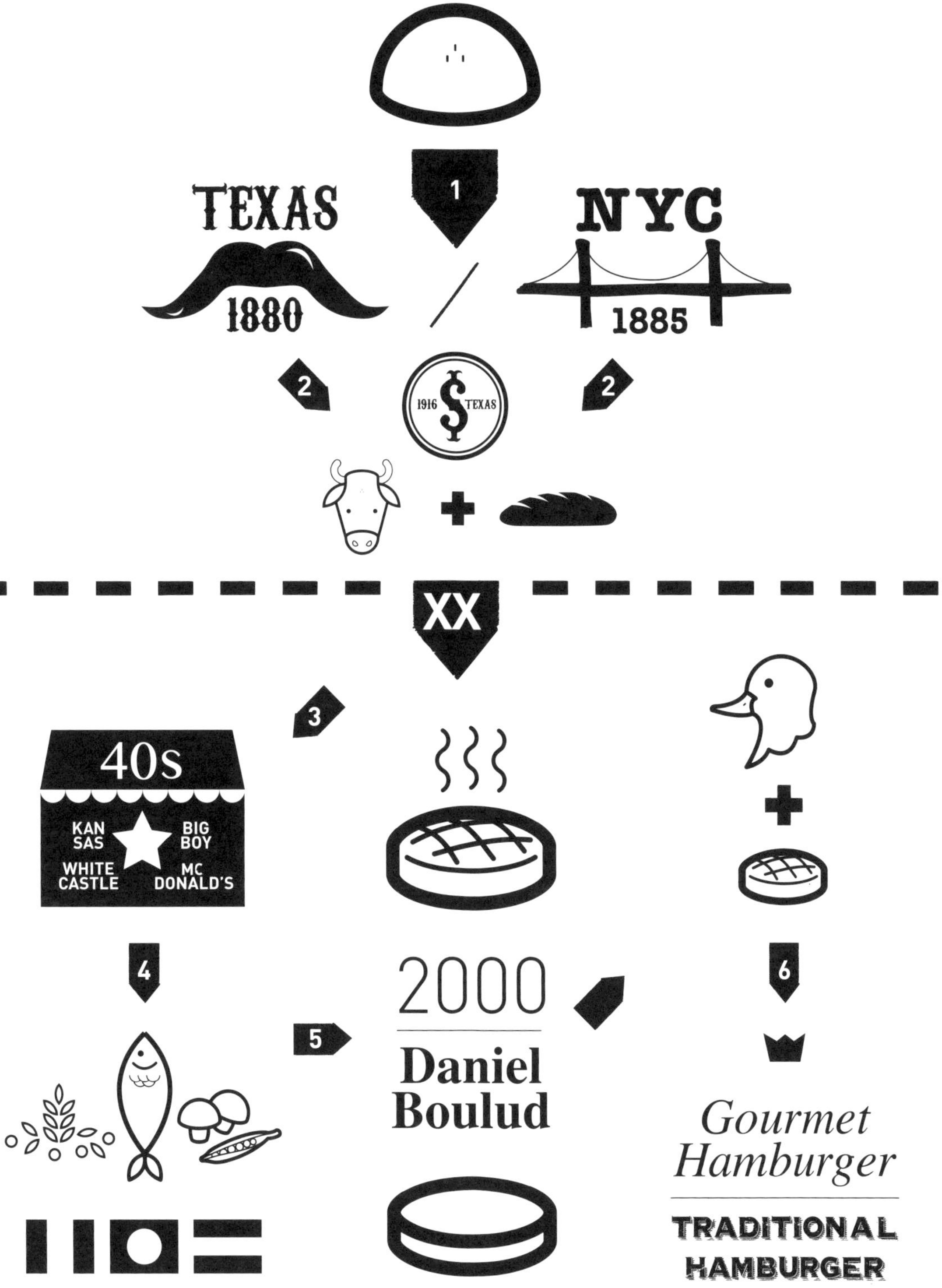

EQUIPMENT

COOKING THE PATTY

Patties have to be cooked on a surface at a very high temperature: the meat needs to be seared so the patties aren't damaged during cooking and to produce the 'Maillard reaction' (named after its inventor)—at high temperatures the whole surface of the patty in contact with the heat source browns and forms a 'crust' due to a chemical reaction between the sugars and amino acids, which adds a great deal of flavour and a unique taste to the meat. You then, ideally, assemble the hamburger on the cooking area so the hamburger can be served hot. To do this, when you reach the point of turning the patties, put the 'heel' and 'crown' of the bun on the cooking area, cut side up, and carry out the assembly of the burger on the heat source.

HOTPLATE

A historical element in the cooking of hamburgers, the hotplate is ideal. Able to reach a very high temperature, it sears food and therefore needs very little fat. You can cook everything on it: sear the patties on one side of the plate, toast the buns and assemble on the other. Usually you can set the thermostat differently depending on the cooking area used. While they are most often found in the garden, there are also hotplates that can be built into the kitchen work surface. An investment you'll never regret ...

GRILL

Grilling (broiling) over heat has a special place in the history of the hamburger, because it gives a particular flavour to the meat: slightly smoky. Hamburgers produced on a grill earn the prestigious description of being 'charbroiled', which some American chains highlight in their logo. Not as even as the hotplate and only to be used for meat, you can also assemble the hamburgers on it if it is large enough.

FRYING PAN

It is entirely possible to make gourmet hamburgers in a frying pan, on one condition: it must be very hot when the patties are added (you don't need to add oil). It is important to coordinate the toasting of the buns before the assembly stage. We recommend that you start toasting the bread just after turning the patties, in the pan if you have the space, otherwise under the grill (broiler).

COOKING THE CHIPS

A deep-fryer is essential for the authentic method, but the oven offers a lighter alternative. Choose a deep-fryer that reaches high temperatures; you will achieve crispier chips. A tip in this regard: it's better to cook smaller quantities in several batches rather than the whole amount at once. This avoids the temperature of the oil dropping too dramatically when the fries are added, which makes them soft.

INTRO / EQUIPMENT

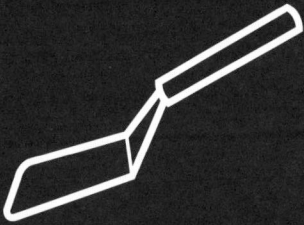

STAINLESS STEEL BOWL

To melt cheese evenly over the patty during cooking, you need to use a stainless steel bowl. After turning the patty, top with the cheese and cover with the bowl for the remaining cooking time. The advantage is being able to melt the cheese while retaining all of the cooking heat inside the spherical bowl. Mastering this technique will take your hamburgers to the next level: melting under a cover changes everything ...

THE TOOLS THAT MAKE THE DIFFERENCE

SOLID SPATULA (OFFSET)

On all the cooking surfaces, the spatula is the key element in cooking and assembling a hamburger. In the United States, it's called a 'hamburger press'. Once you have decided which heat source will be used (pan, grill, hotplate or barbecue), the spatula will play an essential role. First of all, it allows you to handle the patty without damaging it, as it slides just underneath. The patty stays nice and round, in one piece. It also, even if this is a controversial point, allows you to apply even pressure to the patty as it extracts the juice. The ideal is to do this after turning it. The extracted juice cooks and forms a sort of crust, which will give flavour to the patty—the famous Maillard reaction. Finally, the spatula allows you to manoeuvre the bun cooking alongside the patty and assemble the hamburger without running the risk of touching the heat source and burning yourself.

KNIFE OR MINCER

If you decide to mince your own meat, you need good knives, including a paring knife (with a long, thin, flexible blade), useful for trimming unwanted pieces of fat and removing nerves and sinew. Then you take a carving knife, with a more rigid blade, to cut the meat into strips for easier chopping. Make sure you remove all the sinew. If you use a mincer, choose a fairly coarse mincing disc; you will get a more pronounced meat flavour.

TIPS

There is not much you need to know to make a good hamburger.
Here are the main things, which you can add to as your own experience grows.

SPREAD A VERY THIN LAYER OF BUTTER ON THE CUT SIDES OF THE BUN BEFORE YOU BROWN IT IN THE PAN OR UNDER THE GRILL.

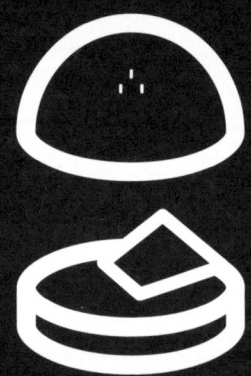

SEASON THE MINCED MEAT WITH SALT AFTER YOU'VE FORMED THE PATTIES: A CRUST WILL FORM DURING COOKING. SEA SALT IS BEST.

TO FORM THE PATTIES BY HAND, IT IS PRACTICAL TO HAVE A BOWL OF LUKEWARM WATER NEXT TO YOUR WORKSPACE: WETTING YOUR FINGERS EACH TIME YOU HANDLE THE PATTIES HELPS WITH SHAPING THE MEAT AND ALLOWS YOU TO ACHIEVE BEAUTIFUL, ROUND AND EVEN PATTIES. A FINAL TIP: MAKE A SMALL HOLLOW IN ONE SIDE OF THE BURGER WITH YOUR THUMB AND START COOKING THE PATTY ON THAT SIDE.

INTRO / TIPS

CUT THE HAMBURGER IN HALF BEFORE
SERVING. TO DO THIS, TAKE A SHARP
KNIFE AND HOLD IT HORIZONTALLY,
BLADE DOWNWARDS, ABOVE THE
BURGER. PUT THE PALM OF YOUR HAND
FLAT ON TOP OF THE BLADE, THEN AIM
AT THE MIDDLE OF THE HAMBURGER
AND CUT FIRMLY, USING YOUR HAND
TO STOP THE HAMBURGER COLLAPSING.

ONLY COOK PATTIES ON A VERY HOT SURFACE, WHETHER A PAN, GRILL, HOTPLATE OR BARBECUE.

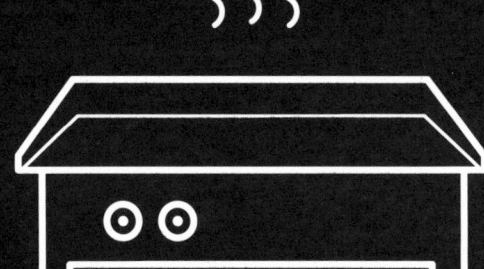

TO SERVE THE HAMBURGERS HOT,
HEAT THE OVEN TO 160°C (315°F/GAS 2–3)
AND PUT THE ASSEMBLED HAMBURGERS IN
THE OVEN FOR 1 MINUTE BEFORE SERVING.

DISSECTION / THE HAMBURGER PIECE BY PIECE

BUN
HAMBURGER BUN

Preparation time: 1 hour + 2.5 hours rising time
Number of buns: 8

strong flour	420 g (15 oz)
dry yeast	10 g (¼ oz)
sugar	40 g (1½ oz)
fine sea salt	1 heaped teaspoon
fermented milk or buttermilk	170 ml (5½ fl oz/⅔ cup)
egg, separated	1
unsalted butter at room temperature	25 g (1 oz)
egg white	1
sesame seeds or poppy seeds	1 large pinch

DOUGH
Put the flour, yeast, sugar and salt in a large mixing bowl. Add the fermented milk, the egg, then the egg yolk. Mix with a wooden spoon or by hand for 3–5 minutes, until you have a uniform dough. Add the butter in pieces and knead for about 15 minutes, until the dough is smooth and supple.

FIRST RISE
Put the dough in an oiled mixing bowl, cover with plastic wrap and allow to rest in a warm place—a turned-off oven with the light on, for example—until the dough has doubled in size, or about 1½ hours.

BUNS
When the dough is ready, put it on a floured work surface. Punch it down to remove the air, then divide into 8 pieces. Roll each piece on the work surface to form perfectly smooth balls. (Don't worry if the first ones aren't perfect, it's an action that takes a little practice.)

SECOND RISE
Put the balls on a baking tray lined with lightly floured baking paper. Cover them loosely with plastic wrap and allow to rise in a warm place for about 1 hour. The buns are ready to bake when you touch them and the fingerprint fills back in very slowly.

BAKING
Preheat the oven to 190°C (375°F/Gas 5). Beat the egg white with a little bit of cold water. Gently, using a soft brush, brush the balls of dough with the mixture and sprinkle with sesame seeds or poppy seeds. Bake for 15–18 minutes, until the buns are golden brown. Allow them to cool before cutting.

FLAVOURS
Replace the milk with vegetable purées if you would like to flavour the buns: tomato, carrot and pumpkin (winter squash) work well.

THE BREAD IS VITAL, WHICH IS WHY WE MAKE IT IN-HOUSE AT BLEND. THIS RECIPE WILL ALLOW YOU TO DISCOVER THE HAMBURGER IN ANOTHER WAY. IT IS THE BREAD THAT KEEPS THE PATTY WARM AND MAINTAINS THE BALANCE OF THE HAMBURGER. THE BOTTOM OF THE HAMBURGER BUN IS CALLED THE 'HEEL' AND THE TOP IS THE 'CROWN'.

CHOICE OF MEAT

It's vital to use fresh meat. You need to include fattier cuts (up to 30% fat): the fat will melt during cooking and leave only its taste, which will lend the patty a particular flavour. When it comes to the cut, we recommend blade (shoulder) and brisket (breast) cuts. You can use a 50/50 combination of these two cuts. That's a 'blend'. You can fashion your own blend depending on the cuts you prefer. Finally, you can also ask your butcher for marbled cuts, which give yet another kind of flavour.

PREPARATION OF THE MEAT: WHOLE PIECES OR MINCED MEAT

If you start with a whole, unminced piece of meat, it is best to cut it up with a knife. The principle is to start by cutting strips, then chop them into dice. Then you form a patty by hand, pressing the meat very hard so the pieces hold together during cooking. Otherwise, use a meat mincer fitted with a coarse mincing disc. Some mixers have a mincing attachment. In the end, if you don't have any of those things, you can ask your butcher to do the job for you.

SHAPING AND SEASONING THE PATTIES

Put a small bowl of lukewarm water next to your workspace. Moistening your fingers regularly to prevent them from sticking to the meat will make it easier to shape the patties. Form the minced meat into balls, keeping your handling of them to a minimum so you don't spoil the freshness of the meat. Make a hollow in the middle of each patty with your thumb or an egg, to allow even cooking through to the middle. Depending on your appetite, you can make patties ranging in size from 100 g (3½ oz) to 170 g (6 oz). Smaller than that and you won't taste the meat, larger than that and your bun won't manage. We recommend a 125 g (4½ oz) patty. Season the patty before cooking, so that the salt forms a crust during cooking.

CREATING PATTIES

To take the recipes a step further, don't hesitate to add vegetables, spices and even other meats to your minced mixtures.

COOKING

The cooking is vital: the meat must be seared over a high heat for a patty that is crusty on the outside and tender inside. After you've turned the patty, press it with a spatula, once only, with a short, sharp action.
BLUE: 2 minutes on each side;
RARE: 3 minutes on each side;
MEDIUM: 4 minutes on each side;
WELL-DONE: 5 minutes on each side.

PATTY
FISH

PATTY n. (plural, **patties**): COMBINATION OF MINCED OR FINELY CHOPPED INGREDIENTS FORMING A SMALL FLAT CAKE.

CHOICE OF FISH

Choosing your fish is the first step in making a good hamburger. We recommend that you go to the fishmonger and be demanding about the piece you take home. It is also preferable to choose firm-fleshed fish, which holds together better during cooking.

PREPARING THE FISH

Fish has a texture that gives you a lot of freedom when it comes to how you prepare your patties.
FILLET: an uncut fish fillet produces a result that's too dense. To make a lighter patty that still retains the texture of the fillet, we recommend slicing the fillet horizontally. Form the patty by laying the slices on top of each other inside a cookie cutter and pressing them together.
CUBES: using a knife, cut the fish into strips, then into small cubes. You can then reassemble them with the help of a cookie cutter, pressing firmly so that the patty holds together. Before cooking, let the patty rest in the refrigerator for a few minutes.
MARINATED: before reassembling the diced fish into patties, you can marinate it in your choice of spices for up to one night in the refrigerator.
CRUMBED: whether your patties are made from sliced or diced fish, you can crumb them (see recipe 27 on page 84).

SALMON

Buy the salmon as a fillet. Cut it horizontally to make 3 slices. If you have a cookie cutter, cut a disc out of each slice (alternatively, use a glass) and then, to form the patty, stack the slices on top of each other. If you want to recreate the patty feel, another option is to cut the salmon into small cubes. Then, form a patty by pressing the pieces very firmly so that they hold together during cooking. The ideal in this case is to let the patty rest in the refrigerator for at least 15 minutes.

COD

Buy the cod as a fillet. Using a cookie cutter, cut out patties the same diameter as the bun. If you don't have a cookie cutter, use a glass in the same way as a cookie cutter, or else put the bun on the cod fillet (wrap the cod in plastic so the bun doesn't absorb any raw fish odour) and, using a knife, cut out a disc of the same diameter.

CHEESE

SOME LIKE IT TASTY, OTHERS WELL MELTED. SOME LIKE BOTH AT THE SAME TIME. TO ACHIEVE THIS, IT IS A GOOD IDEA TO KNOW A BIT ABOUT CHEESE AND THE MOST SUCCESSFUL PAIRINGS. NOT ALL CHEESES ARE BETTER WHEN MELTED AND NOT ALL CHEESES GO WELL WITH BEEF.

BLUE

The bitterness of a blue cheese depends on its concentration of mould. It is perfect in a sauce, melted into relishes or crumbled on top of the patty. There are different kinds of blue cheese: French Roquefort, Italian Gorgonzola … Blue cheese goes very well with onions.

CHEDDAR

The most universal of cheeses, originating in England. Contrary to popular belief, it does not melt well and can even release fat when cooked. It has a remarkable flavour, however, and adds a lot of taste to a hamburger. Choose orange cheddar for easier melting; white aged cheddar needs to be worked more to melt well. Cheddar goes very well with everything.

GOAT'S CHEESE

With a fresh taste that ranges from a mild to a very pronounced flavour on the palate as it matures, goat's cheese pairs very well with raw vegetables, or sweet-and-savoury dishes. It loses some of its bitterness when melted.

FETA

The Greek cheese par excellence. There are many varieties, varying in firmness and strength of flavour. This cheese does not really melt, but it adds an interesting bitterness to vegetable-based preparations. Feta goes very well with most raw vegetables. It's a cheese that adds freshness.

GOUDA

From nutty to sharp, depending on its age, gouda goes well with spices and melts easily.

GRUYÈRE

Originating in Switzerland, Gruyère is widely consumed in France, where it is used in many pasta-based dishes. There are several varieties, with higher or lower fat contents. The younger cheeses are creamy and melt well, the older ones become grainy and have a more pronounced taste. Gruyère goes very well with beef.

MOZZARELLA

A mild and very fresh Italian cheese whose taste varies between the flavour of the

RELISH

AT BLEND, THE HAMBURGERS MAKE YOU REALISE THAT VEGETABLES HAVE FLAVOUR. BRAISING AND STEWING FINELY CHOPPED VEGETABLES AND FRUIT OPENS UP A FIELD OF INFINITE POSSIBILITIES. EVERYTHING IS PERMITTED: COMBINE VEGETABLES, FRUITS AND SPICES ACCORDING TO YOUR TASTES AND GIVE FREE REIN TO YOUR CREATIVITY.

HERE ARE THREE EXAMPLES THAT SHOW YOU THE TECHNIQUE AND WHICH YOU CAN USE AS INSPIRATION FOR MAKING YOUR OWN RELISHES.

ONION RELISH WITH BALSAMIC VINEGAR

Preparation time: 45 mins
To fill 4 hamburgers

brown onions, thinly sliced	4
butter	1 small knob
caster (superfine) sugar	1 tablespoon
balsamic vinegar	50 ml (1¾ fl oz)

Sauté the onions in the butter in a saucepan until lightly browned. Sprinkle with the sugar and caramelise slightly. Deglaze with the balsamic vinegar. Wait until the vinegar has completely evaporated and cook gently over low heat for 20 minutes, stirring constantly.

APPLE–SHALLOT RELISH

Preparation time: 35 mins
To fill 4 hamburgers

granny smith apples	2
French shallots, finely chopped	4
water	50 ml (1¾ fl oz)
caster (superfine) sugar	50 g (1¾ oz)

Peel the apples and cut into pieces, removing the core. In a saucepan, sauté the apples and shallots over low heat. Cook for about 25 minutes, stirring regularly and incorporating the water and sugar gradually.

PARSNIP–SPRING ONION RELISH

Preparation time: 40 mins
To fill 4 hamburgers

parsnips	4 small
bulb spring onions (scallions), chopped	2
water	125 ml (4 fl oz/½ cup)
caster (superfine) sugar	50 g (1¾ oz)

Using a mandolin, thinly slice the parsnip. In a saucepan, sauté the parsnips and onions over low heat. Cook for about 30–35 minutes, or until the parsnips have softened, stirring regularly and incorporating the water and sugar gradually.

SALAD LEAVES

SALAD LEAVES ARE A FUNDAMENTAL ELEMENT OF A HAMBURGER: IT'S THE ELEMENT THAT CAN ADD CRISPNESS, FLAVOUR AND FRESHNESS.

Before choosing a leaf, remember that you can replace it with crunchy or fried vegetables, such as sliced red radish, daikon or fennel. Here are the salad leaves that are particularly well suited to hamburgers:

ENDIVE: for a touch of bitterness.

ICEBERG: for freshness and crunchiness. It can be eaten raw or cooked.

MÂCHE: recommended for all vegetarian burgers. It is eaten raw.

MESCLUN: for a combination of flavours. It contains at least five varieties of salad leaf (lettuce, mâche, rocket (arugula), witlof (chicory), radicchio, escarole).

BABY SPINACH: for an enjoyable flavour.

COS LETTUCE: for its freshness.

ROCKET (ARUGULA): for its peppery taste. It can be eaten raw or cooked. It is best used in moderation as it has a strong flavour, even after cooking.

BABY COS LETTUCE: for its sweetness.

RADICCHIO TREVISO: for its slightly tart flavour. It can be eaten raw or cooked. Because of its colour, it adds a decorative touch to the hamburger.

To prepare salad leaves, simply wash them. To take them a step further, don't hesitate to add spices or dress them.

SAUCE

THERE ARE A FEW PILLARS THAT HOLD UP THOUSANDS OF HAMBURGER RECIPES ACROSS THE WORLD. YOU CAN AVOID THE COMMON SHORT CUT OF BUYING THEM READY-MADE, ESPECIALLY IF YOU WANT TO CUSTOMISE THEM TO YOUR OWN TASTE: SWEETER, SALTIER OR SPICIER. THESE SAUCES HAVE BECOME LEGENDS. MAKE YOUR OWN BURGERS LEGENDARY.

BARBECUE

Preparation time: 25 mins

vinegar	50 ml (1¾ fl oz)
tomato sauce (ketchup)	240 ml (8 fl oz)
water	240 ml (8 fl oz)
worcestershire sauce	1 tablespoon
raw (demerara) sugar	115 g (4 oz)
onion, chopped	½
salt	1 teaspoon
pepper	¼ teaspoon
butter	20 g (¾ oz)
Tabasco sauce	a few drops
celery seeds	¼ teaspoon

Combine all the ingredients in a saucepan and cook over low heat for 15 minutes, stirring regularly.

CHIPOTLE

Preparation time: 30 mins

onion, chopped	1 small
garlic	1 clove
tomato sauce (ketchup)	250 ml (9 fl oz/1 cup)
marinated chipotle peppers	40 g (1½ oz)
cider vinegar	50 ml (1¾ fl oz)
brown sugar	80 g (2¾ oz)
water	250 ml (9 fl oz/1 cup)

Put all the ingredients in a saucepan over medium heat and stir. Cook for 30 minutes. Process the mixture until you have a smooth and uniform texture. (Chipotle peppers marinated in Adobo sauce are available in supermarkets.)

TOMATO

Preparation time: 2 hours 40 mins

tomatoes, chopped	1 kg (2 lb 4 oz)
onions, chopped	2
garlic, crushed	1 clove
cloves (whole)	1 teaspoon
paprika	1 pinch
salt	1 teaspoon
pepper	1 teaspoon
sugar	200 g (7 oz)
vinegar	200 ml (7 fl oz)

Put the tomatoes, onions, garlic, cloves, paprika, salt and pepper into a heavy-based frying pan. Simmer for 1½ hours over low heat, crushing the tomatoes halfway through the cooking. Add the sugar and vinegar and cook for a further 1½ hours, until the mixture is thick. Process the sauce then put the mixture through a fine sieve. Pour the strained sauce in a saucepan and reduce over low heat for 1 hour. Keep the sauce in jars.

GARLIC MAYONNAISE

Preparation time: 15 mins

egg yolk	1
mustard	1 teaspoon
salt	1 pinch
olive oil	200 ml (7 fl oz)
garlic	2 cloves

Whisk the egg yolk with the mustard and salt. Gradually incorporate the oil. Peel the garlic and crush it into the mayonnaise. Stir. Ideally allow the mayonnaise to stand for 1 hour in the refrigerator.

CHIPS
POTATO / SWEET POTATO / PARSNIP

IN THE DEEP-FRYER

Preparation time: 30 mins
Number of serves: 4

bintje (yellow finn) potatoes, sweet
potatoes or parsnips .... **1 kg (2 lb 4 oz)**
oil .... **for deep-frying**

IN THE OVEN

Preparation time: 1 hour
Number of serves: 4

sweet potatoes
.... **5, about 750 g (1 lb 10 oz)**
olive oil .... **3 tablespoons**
garlic, chopped .... **1 clove**
lemon (juice) .... **½**
salt .... **2 teaspoons**
freshly ground black pepper ... **½ teaspoon**
paprika .... **½ teaspoon**
basil, chopped .... **2 tablespoons**

IN THE DEEP-FRYER

Cut the potatoes into sticks about 5 mm (¼ inch) wide, sweet potatoes into sticks about 1 cm (½ inch) wide, and parsnips into sticks about 1.5 cm (⅝ inch) wide. Plunge the chips into the oil heated to 140°C (275°F) for 5 minutes. Drain. Before assembling the hamburgers, plunge the chips into the oil heated to 180°C (350°F) for 3 minutes to brown them. Drain on paper towels to remove excess oil.

IN THE OVEN: SWEET POTATO

Peel the potatoes and cut into long chips about 1 cm (½ inch) wide. Preheat the oven to 200°C (400°F/Gas 6). Put the chips in a resealable plastic bag. Add the olive oil, garlic, lemon juice, salt, pepper and paprika. Shake the bag to coat the chips with the oil and spices. Brush the baking tray with olive oil. Spread the chips out evenly on the tray. Bake for about 45 minutes, until they are golden brown. Remove from the oven. Season with salt and sprinkle with the basil. These sweet potato chips go very well with the garlic mayonnaise.

CHIPS NEED TO BE TAKEN SERIOUSLY IN ORDER TO BE GOOD. TO ENSURE THAT THEY ARE CRISP ON THE OUTSIDE AND TENDER ON THE INSIDE, THERE ARE TWO THINGS TO WATCH. THE FIRST IS THE CUT, THE SECOND IS THE TEMPERATURE OF THE OIL. WHEN CUTTING UP POTATOES, MAKE SURE THE WIDTH IS NOT MORE THAN 1 CM (½ INCH) AND MAKE THE CHIPS EVEN. THE MORE POWERFUL THE DEEP-FRYER, THE MORE QUICKLY THE TEMPERATURE OF THE OIL RISES AFTER IMMERSING THE CHIPS, AND THE BETTER THEY SEAL, WHICH IS IDEAL. MAKE SURE YOU PAY ATTENTION TO THE TEMPERATURES.

1 \

PURE / 100% FISH OR MEAT

RECIPE NO. 1

BASE
THE CLASSIC HAMBURGER

Level of difficulty:
Preparation time: 30 mins
Number of hamburgers: 4

Type of meat

BEEF

BUNS
| homemade or bought buns | 4 |

PATTIES
| beef, minced (ground) | 500 g (1 lb 2 oz) |
| sea salt | a few pinches |

SAUCE 1
brown onions, diced	2
olive oil	1 drizzle
tomato passata (puréed tomatoes)	30 ml (1 fl oz)
herbes de Provence	1 teaspoon
salt	1 pinch
pepper	1 pinch

SAUCE 2
| gherkins (pickles), diced | 4 large |
| honey mayonnaise (see page 106) | 30 ml (1 fl oz) |

TOPPINGS
| iceberg lettuce | ½ |

BUNS
Make the buns as described on page 14 or use ready-made buns.

PATTIES
Form 4 patties from the minced beef and season them with the sea salt.

SAUCES
Divide the onion into two equal piles. Combine the gherkins and half the onion with the sweet mustard and set aside in the refrigerator. Sauté the rest of the onion with a little olive oil until softened and add the tomato passata and herbes de Provence. Season with salt and pepper.

COOKING THE PATTIES
Cook the patties in a hot frying pan over high heat, 3 minutes per side for rare patties.

ASSEMBLY
Cut buns in half horizontally and toast them for 2 minutes under the grill (broiler). Cut the iceberg lettuce into 4 slices. Spread the cut side of the bun heels and crowns with the honey mayonnaise. Put the patties on the heel, followed by the iceberg lettuce and the tomato sauce with herbs and onion. Top with the crowns.

RECIPE NO. 2

BAKE
THE CLASSIC WITH BACON

Level of difficulty:
Preparation time: 35 mins
Number of hamburgers: 4

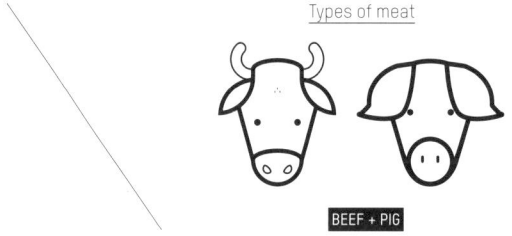
Types of meat

BEEF + PIG

BUNS
homemade or bought buns 4

PATTIES
beef, minced (ground) .... **500 g (1 lb 2 oz)**
sea salt .... **a few pinches**

RELISH
tomato, finely diced 1
onion, finely diced .... ½
gherkins (pickles), finely diced 1
bacon, rind and excess fat removed, finely diced
.... **4 slices**
oregano .... **1 pinch**
cheddar cheese, cut into small pieces
.... **140 g (5 oz/1 cup)**
water .... **125 ml (4 fl oz/½ cup)**

SAUCE
tomato sauce (ketchup)
.... **80 ml (2½ fl oz/⅓ cup)**

TOPPINGS
iceberg lettuce, sliced .... ½

BUNS
Make the buns as described on page 14 or use ready-made buns.

PATTIES
Form 4 patties from the minced beef and season them with the sea salt.

RELISH
Put the tomato, onion and gherkins in separate bowls. Sauté the bacon in a frying pan. When it is well browned, add the tomatoes and oregano. Fry for 2 minutes then set aside in a bowl. Put the cheddar in a separate bowl with the water and heat in a microwave oven for three 20-second bursts. Remove from the microwave and stir; the mixture should be melting, but not too runny. Add the bacon mixture and the diced onion and gherkin to make a smooth mixture.

COOKING THE PATTIES
Cook the patties in a hot frying pan over high heat, 3 minutes per side for rare patties.

ASSEMBLY
Cut the buns in half horizontally and toast them for 2 minutes under the grill (broiler). Spread the cut side of the bun heels and crowns with the tomato sauce. Put the patties on the heels, pour over the cheddar relish, add the iceberg lettuce and top with the crowns.

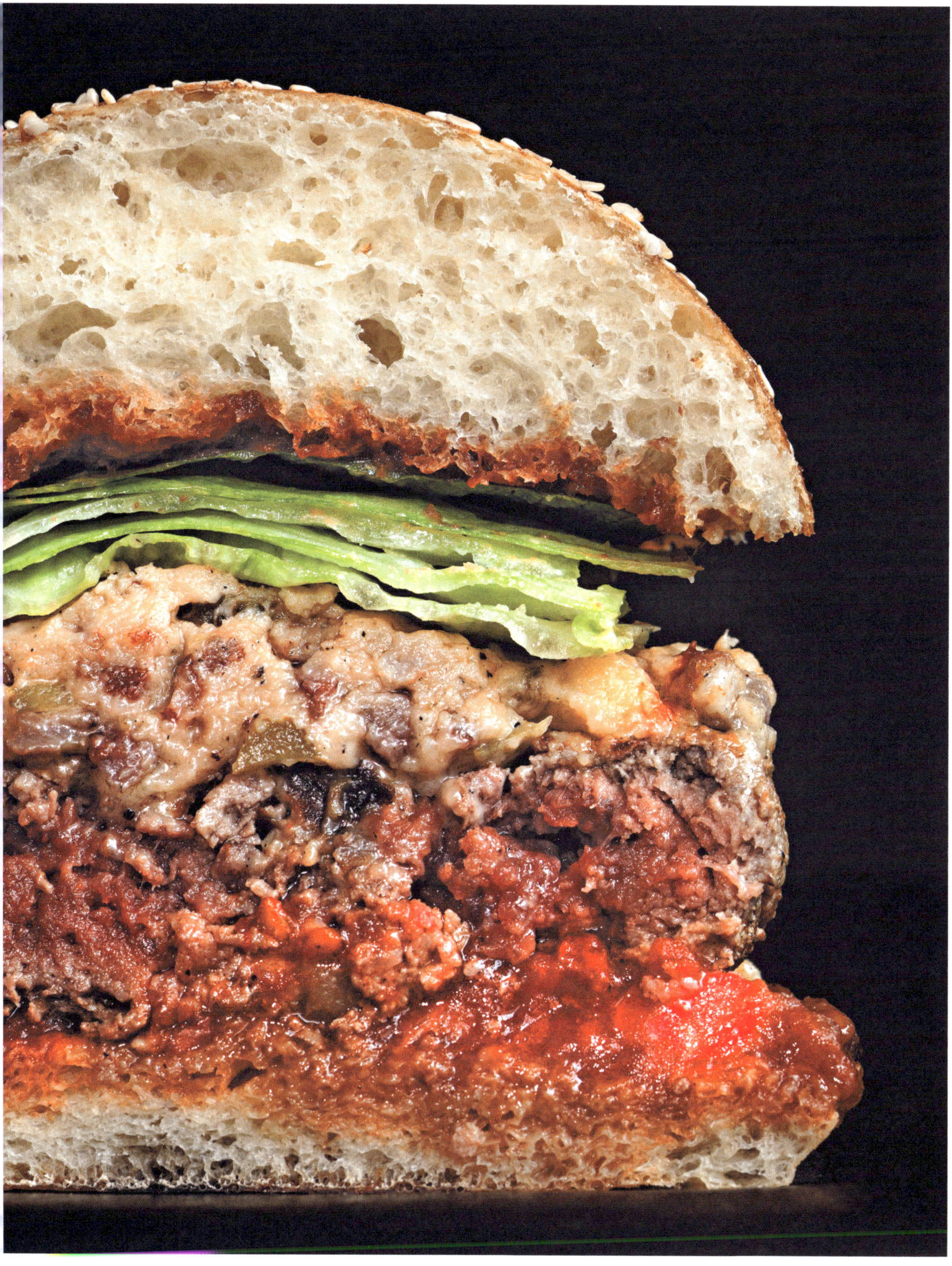

RECIPE NO. 3

BRIE
BRIE DE MEAUX, WHOLEGRAIN MUSTARD

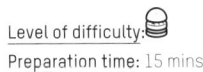

Level of difficulty:
Preparation time: 15 mins
Number of hamburgers: 4

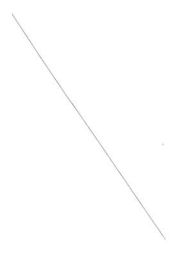

Type of meat

BEEF

BUNS
homemade or bought buns	4

PATTIES
beef, minced (ground)	500 g (1 lb 2 oz)
sea salt	a few pinches

RELISH
onion, finely chopped	1
honey	50 g (1¾ oz)

CHEESE
small brie cheeses	2 × 125 g (4½ oz)
wholegrain mustard	150 g (5½ oz)
dry breadcrumbs	50 g (1¾ oz)

TOPPINGS
iceberg lettuce, shredded	½

BUNS
Make the buns as described on page 14 or use ready-made buns.

PATTIES
Form 4 patties from the minced beef and season them with the sea salt.

RELISH
Sauté the onion in a saucepan with the honey over high heat for about 5 minutes until caramelised.

CHEESE
Preheat the oven to 180°C (350°F/Gas 4). Cut each small brie in half horizontally to make 4 rounds. Put them on a baking tray, cut side up. Spread each round with wholegrain mustard (reserving a little for the assembly stage), then sprinkle with the breadcrumbs to make an even layer. Put in the oven for 5 minutes.

COOKING THE PATTIES
Cook the patties in a hot frying pan over high heat, 3 minutes per side for rare patties. Put the slices of brie, breadcrumb sides up, on the patties.

ASSEMBLY
Cut the buns in half horizontally and toast them for 2 minutes under the grill (broiler). Spread the cut side of the bun heels with mustard, add the caramelised onions, the patties with the brie and finish with the shredded lettuce. Top with the crowns.

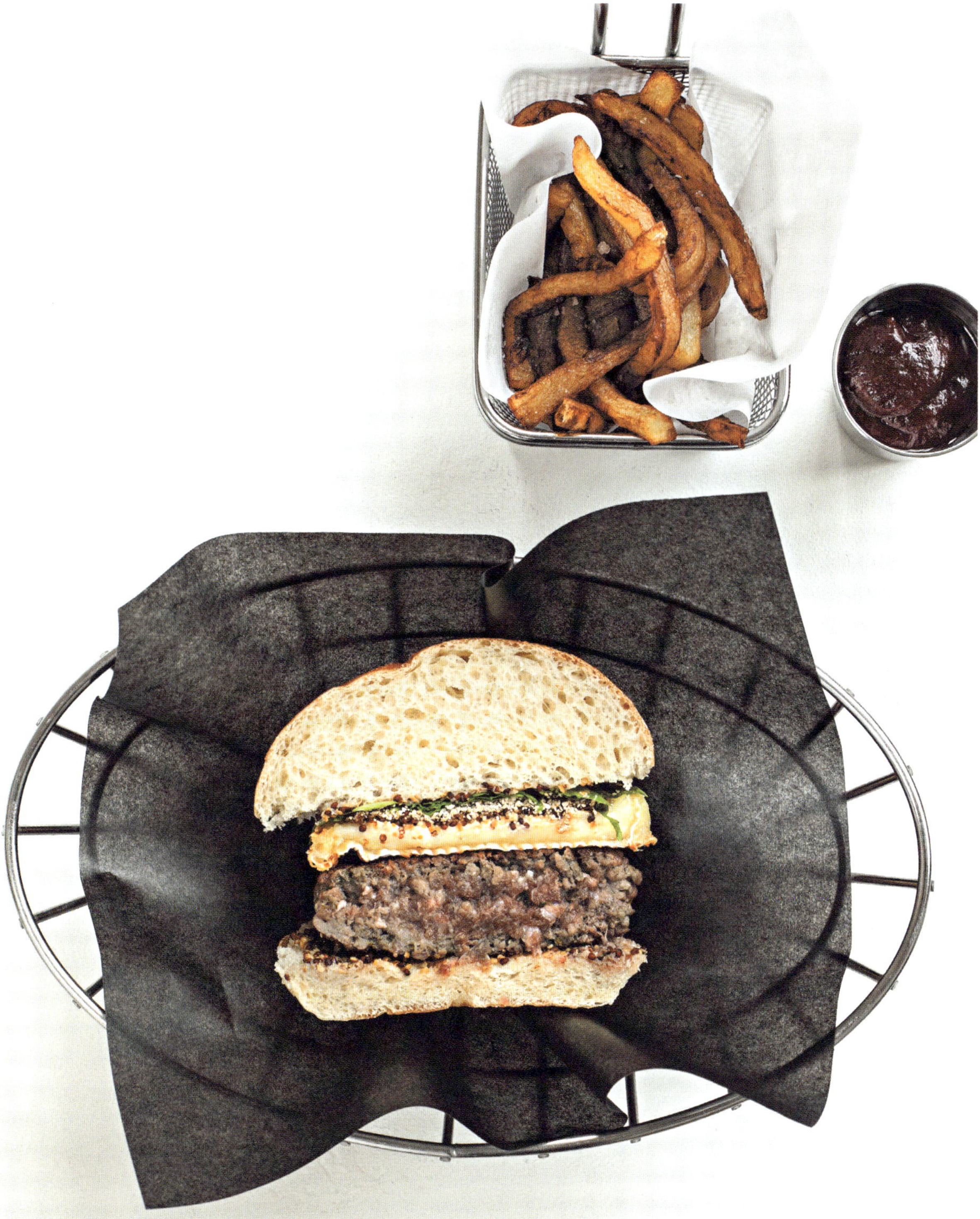

RECIPE NO. 4

FETA
BEEF, TOMATO–FETA

Level of difficulty:
Preparation time: 30 mins
Number of hamburgers: 4

Type of meat

BEEF

BUNS
homemade or bought buns	4

PATTIES
beef, minced (ground)	500 g (1 lb 2 oz)
sea salt	a few pinches

TOPPINGS
feta cheese	80 g (2¾ oz)
tomato, finely diced	1
chives, snipped	15–20 g (½–¾ oz)
lemon (juice)	1

SAUCE
fresh mint, chopped	20 g (¾ oz)
crème fraîche	100 g (3½ oz)
salt	1 pinch
pepper	1 pinch

BUNS
Make the buns as described on page 14 or use ready-made buns.

PATTIES
Form 4 patties from the minced beef and season them with the sea salt.

TOPPINGS
Put the feta in a microwave oven for 20 seconds to soften. Combine the tomato and feta, season with salt and pepper. Add the chives and lemon juice.

SAUCE
Combine the mint with the crème fraîche, season with salt and pepper.

COOKING THE PATTIES
Cook the patties in a hot frying pan over high heat, 3 minutes per side for rare patties.

ASSEMBLY
Cut the buns in half horizontally and toast them for 2 minutes under the grill (broiler). Spread the cut side of the bun heels with the mint cream, add the patties, spread with more mint crème fraîche, then the tomato-feta mixture. Top with the crowns.

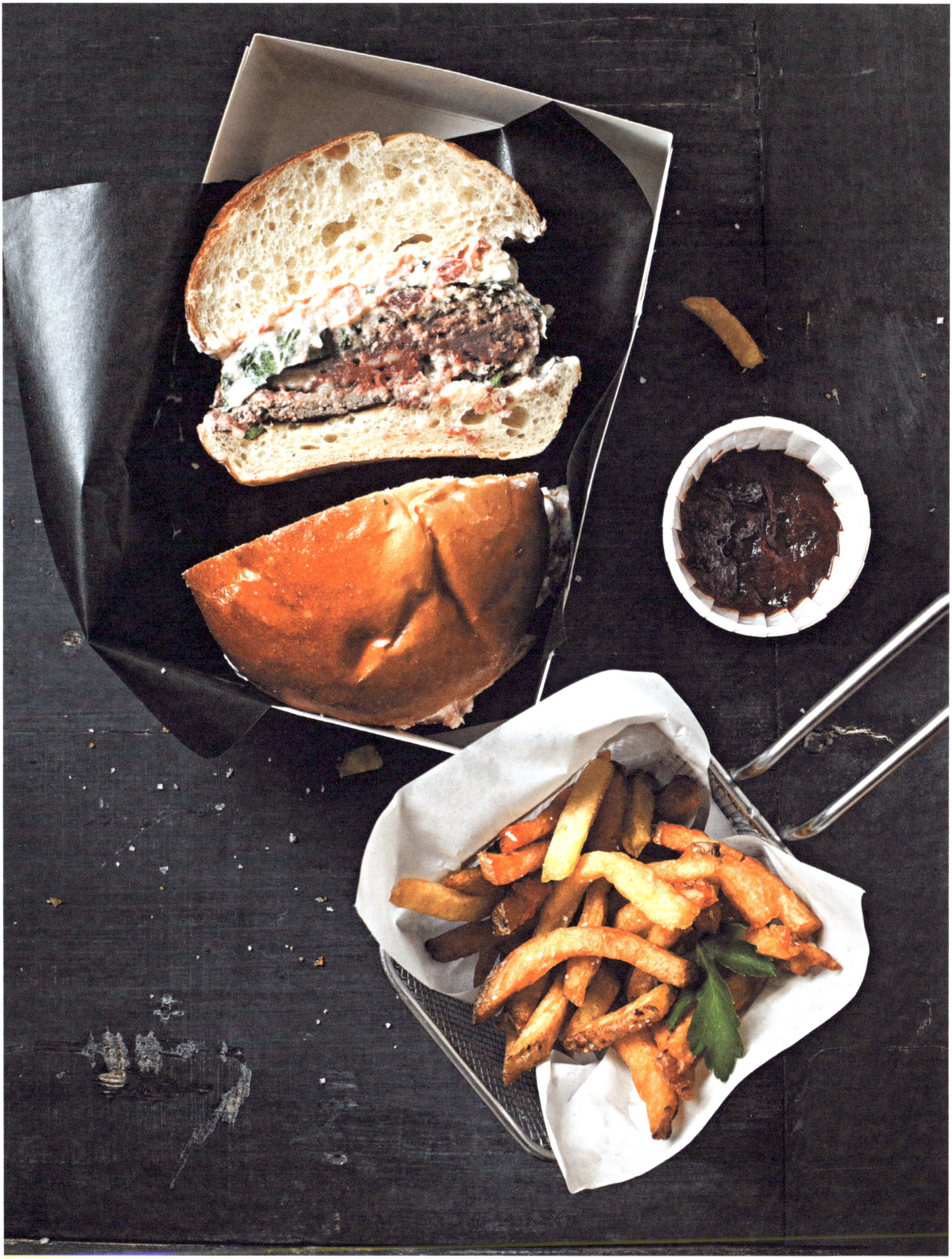

RECIPE NO. 5

MOZZA
BEEF, MOZZARELLA, PESTO

Level of difficulty:
Preparation time: 20 mins
Number of hamburgers: 4

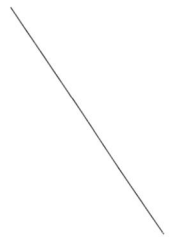

Type of meat

BEEF

BUNS
homemade or bought buns 4

PATTIES
beef, minced (ground) .... **500 g (1 lb 2 oz)**
sea salt .... 1 pinch

PESTO
basil .... 1 bunch
pine nuts .... 15 g (½ oz)
parmesan cheese, finely grated
.... 30 g (1 oz)
garlic .... 1 clove
olive oil .... 2 tablespoons

TOPPINGS
buffalo mozzarella cheese, cut into thin slices 1
small semi-dried tomatoes, coarsely chopped 10
salt .... 1 pinch
pepper .... 1 pinch
basil leaves .... ½ bunch

BUNS
Make the buns as described on page 14 or use ready-made buns.

PATTIES
Form 4 patties from the minced beef and season them with the sea salt.

PESTO
Pluck the basil leaves and put them in a food processor. Add the pine nuts, parmesan, garlic and olive oil, then process everything together.

COOKING THE PATTIES
Cook the patties in a hot frying pan over high heat. Turn the patties after 3 minutes, top them with the mozzarella, season with salt and pepper and cover them with a stainless steel bowl. Cook for a further 3 minutes until the mozzarella has melted.

ASSEMBLY
Cut the buns in half horizontally and toast them for 2 minutes under the grill (broiler). Spread the cut side of the bun heels with the pesto, add the pieces of semi-dried tomato, then the patties with mozzarella and the basil leaves. Top with the crowns.

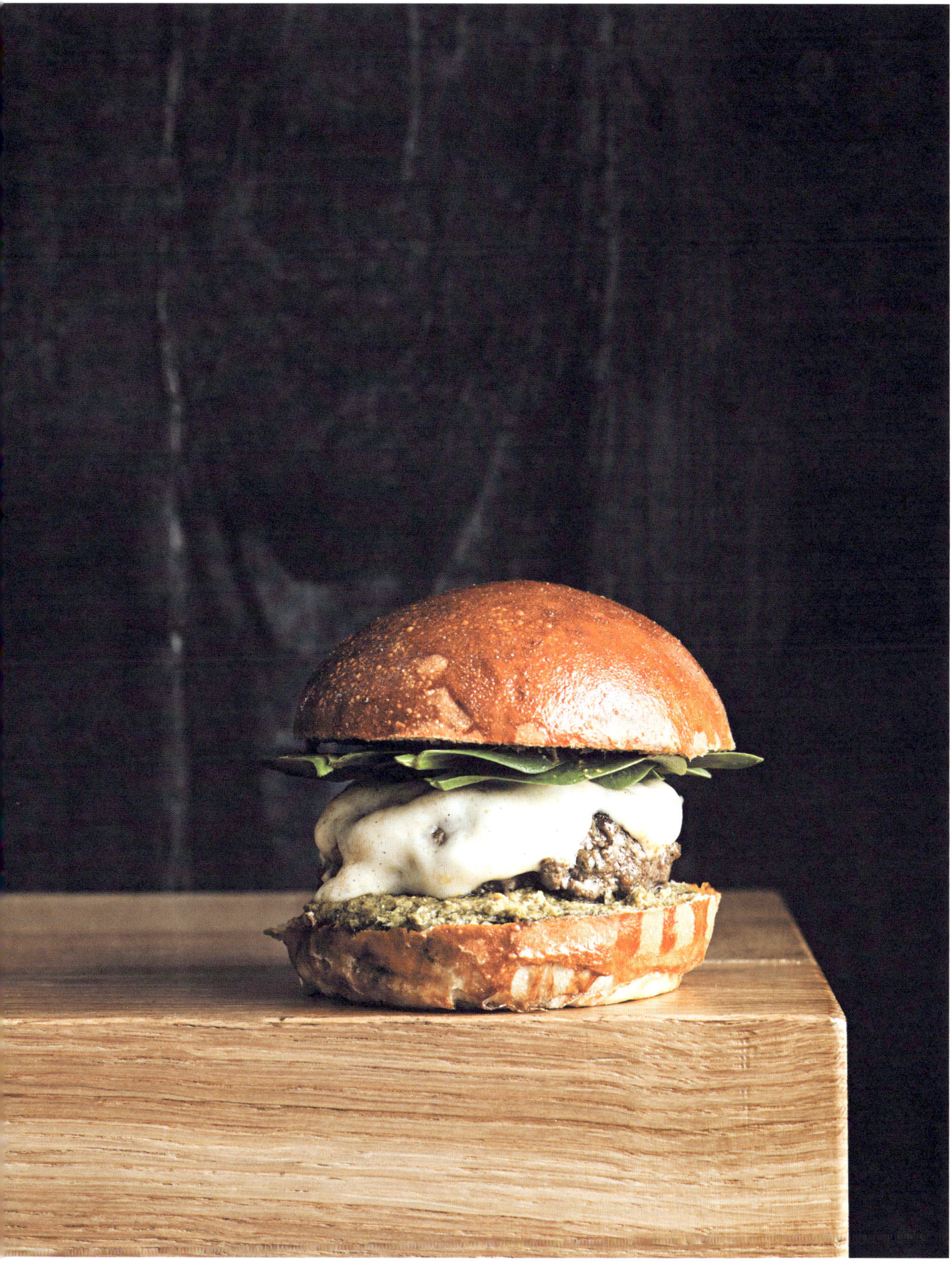

RECIPE NO. 6

CHERRY

BEEF, SHEEP'S MILK CHEESE, CHERRY JAM

Level of difficulty:
Preparation time: 25 mins
Number of hamburgers: 4

Type of meat

BEEF

BUNS
homemade or bought buns … 4

PATTIES
beef, minced (ground) … **500 g (1 lb 2 oz)**
sea salt … **1 pinch**

RELISH
sheep's milk cheese, cut into small cubes … **100 g (3½ oz)**
cherry jam … **80 g (2¾ oz/¼ cup)**

TOPPINGS
iceberg lettuce, shredded … ½

BUNS
Make the buns as described on page 14 or use ready-made buns.

PATTIES
Form 4 patties from the minced beef and season them with the sea salt.

RELISH
Mix the cubes of cheese with half of the cherry jam in a bowl. Reserve the remaining cherry jam for serving.

COOKING THE PATTIES
Cook the patties in a hot frying pan over high heat, 3 minutes per side. Before finishing the cooking, spread half of the cheese-cherry relish over them and cover with a stainless steel bowl so that the temperature rises and the cheese begins to melt.

ASSEMBLY
Cut the buns in half horizontally and toast them for 2 minutes under the grill (broiler). Spread the cut side of the bun heels with the remaining cheese-cherry relish, then put the patties topped with relish and the lettuce on top. Finish with the crowns, spread with the reserved cherry jam.

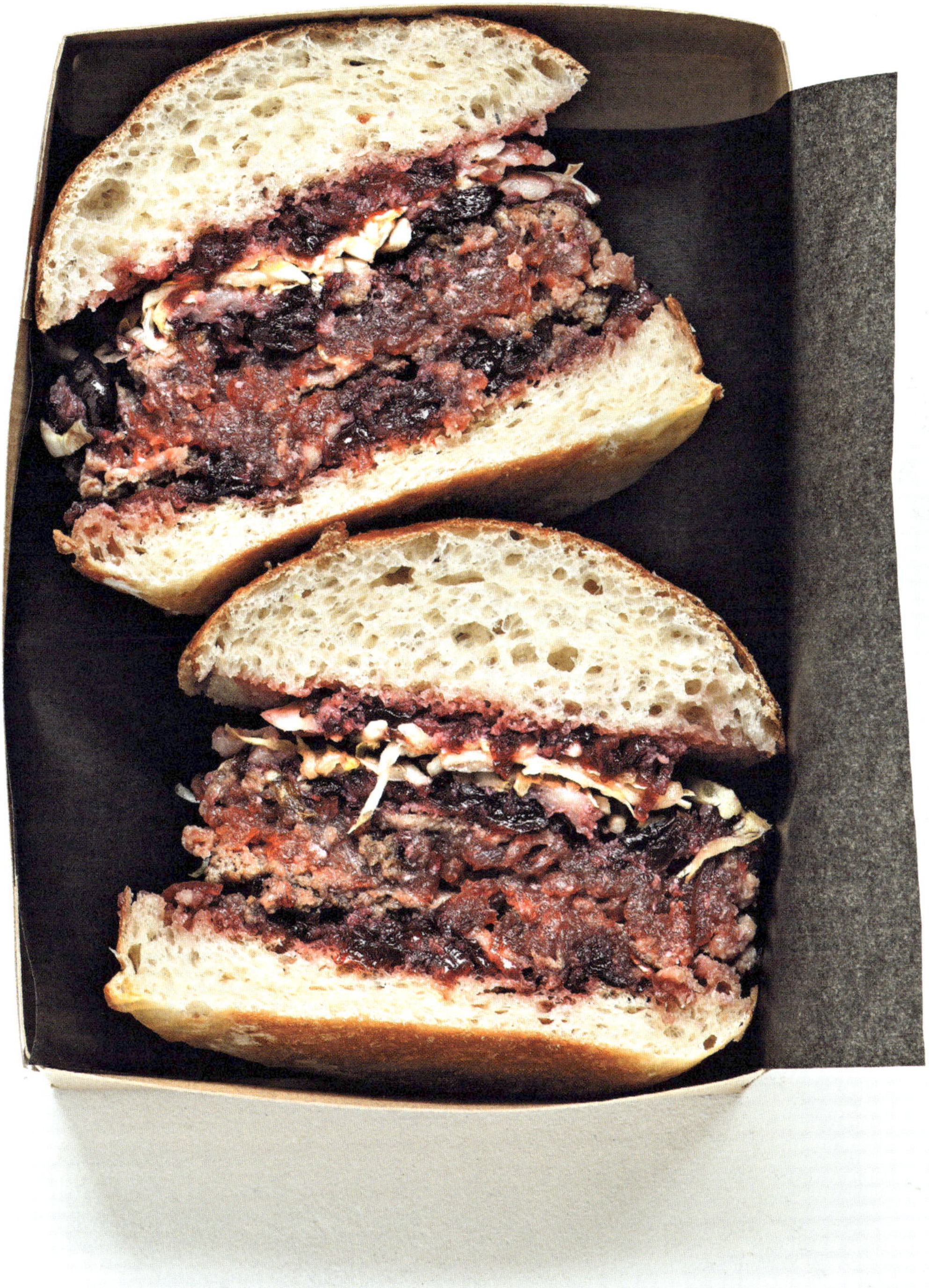

RECIPE NO. 7

CANTAL
BEEF, CANTAL, FIG-GRAPE RELISH

Level of difficulty:
Preparation time: 2 hours
Number of hamburgers: 4

Type of meat

BEEF

BUNS
homemade or bought buns	4

PATTIES
beef, minced (ground)	500 g (1 lb 2 oz)
sea salt	a few pinches

RELISH
figs	100 g (3½ oz)
granulated sugar	150 g (5½ oz)
white grapes	100 g (3½ oz)
lemon	1
olive oil	a splash
French shallots, thinly sliced	3
caster sugar	50 g (1¾ oz)
balsamic vinegar	1 tablespoon

CARROT CHIPS
carrot	1
plain (all-purpose) flour	2 or 3 pinches
salt	1 pinch
pepper	1 pinch
ground cumin	1 pinch
olive oil	80 ml (2½ fl oz/⅓ cup)

TOPPINGS
Cantal or mature cheddar cheese, cut into small cubes	120 g (4¼ oz)
iceberg lettuce, shredded	¼

BUNS
Make the buns as described on page 14 or use ready-made buns.

PATTIES
Form 4 patties from the minced beef and season them with the sea salt.

RELISH
Wash the figs, cut them into 8, removing any hard parts. Put them in a bowl with the granulated sugar. Wash and remove the stalks from the grapes. Peel and remove the seeds (cut the grapes in half to make this operation easier). Add the grapes to the figs. Wash the lemon and remove the zest in 5 mm (¼ inch) strips using a vegetable peeler. Dice the lemon pulp, discarding the seeds and pith. Add the zest and pulp to the fruit and gently combine. Pour the mixture into a pan. Cook for 25 minutes, or until jammy, over a low heat, stirring occasionally: do not let the jam brown. Remove the lemon zest at the end of the cooking. Heat the olive oil in a frying pan over low heat and sauté the shallots. When they start to brown, add the caster sugar and balsamic vinegar and stir to combine. Incorporate the shallots into the fig-grape jam and stir until the mixture is combined, then remove from the heat.

CARROT CHIPS
Wash and peel the carrot, cut it into rounds and put them into a resealable plastic bag. Add the flour, salt, pepper, cumin and 2 tablespoons of the olive oil. Close the bag and shake so that all the carrot slices are coated with the mixture. Sauté the slices in the remaining oil in a frying pan until they become crispy, or cook briefly in a deep-fryer.

COOKING THE PATTIES
Cook the patties in a hot frying pan over high heat, 3 minutes per side for rare patties.

ASSEMBLY
Cut the buns in half horizontally and toast them for 2 minutes under the grill (broiler). Combine the cubes of Cantal cheese with the relish. Spread the cut side of the bun heels and crowns with some relish and top with the patties, carrot chips, more relish and shredded lettuce. Finish with the crowns.

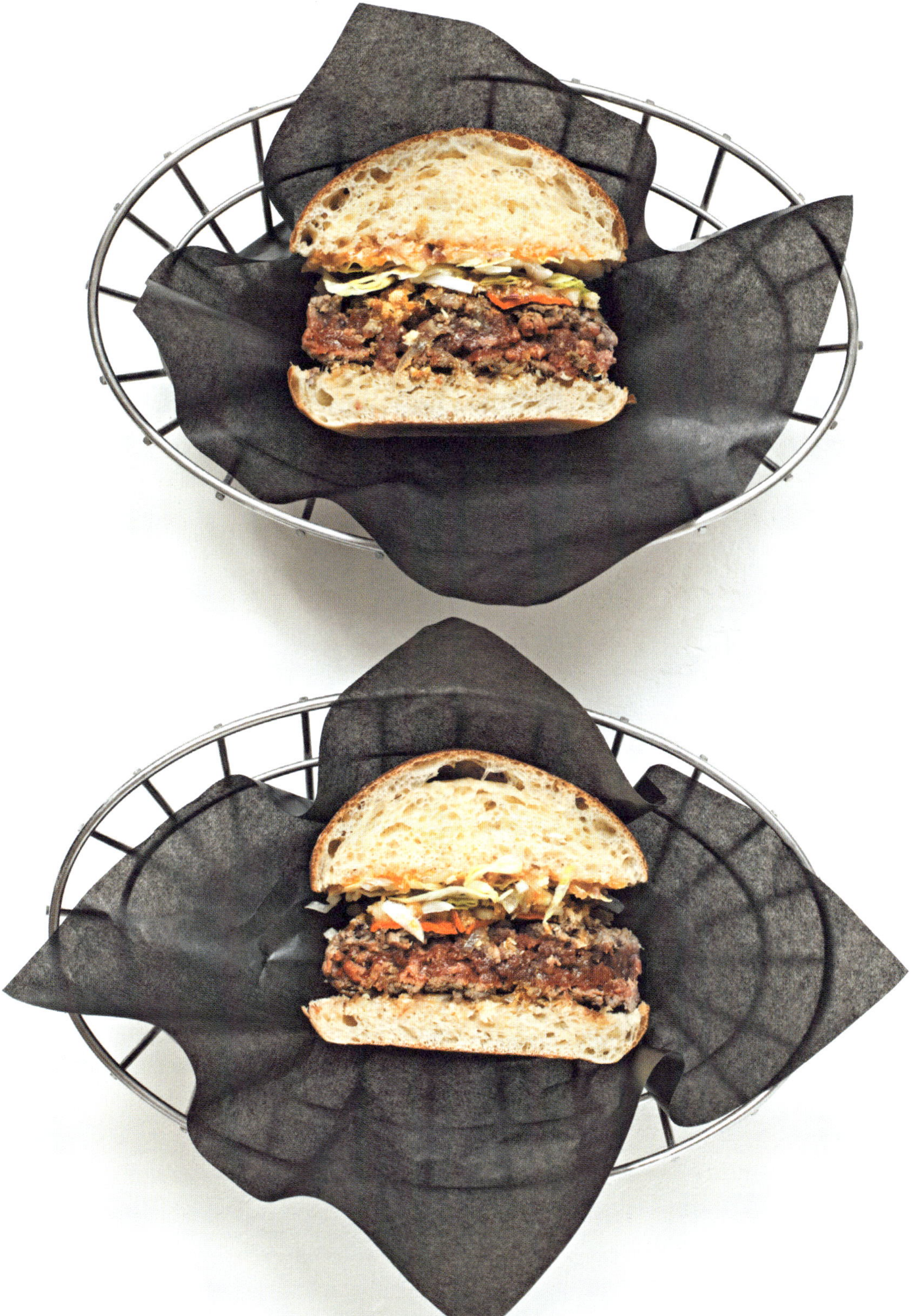

RECIPE NO. 8

MUSH

BEEF, MUSHROOMS

Level of difficulty:
Preparation time: 25 mins
Number of hamburgers: 4

Type of meat

BEEF

BUNS
homemade or bought buns 4

PATTIES
beef, minced (ground) .... **500 g (1 lb 2 oz)**
sea salt .... **a few pinches**

RELISH
Swiss brown or portobello mushrooms, sliced
.... **7, about 200 g (7 oz)**
onion, sliced .... **1 large**
olive oil .... **1 drizzle**
thin (pouring) cream .... **120 ml (4 fl oz)**

TOPPINGS
iceberg lettuce, shredded .... **¼**

BUNS
Make the buns as described on page 14 or use ready-made buns.

PATTIES
Form 4 patties from the minced beef and season them with the sea salt.

RELISH
Sauté the mushrooms and onion with the olive oil in a frying pan. Once the mixture is coloured, add the cream and reduce over low heat for about 8–10 minutes. Season.

COOKING THE PATTIES
Cook the patties in a hot frying pan over high heat, 3 minutes per side for rare patties.

ASSEMBLY
Cut the buns in half horizontally and toast them for 2 minutes under the grill (broiler). Spread the cut side of the bun heels with half of the mushroom sauce then top with the patties and the remaining sauce. Add the iceberg lettuce and finish with the crowns.

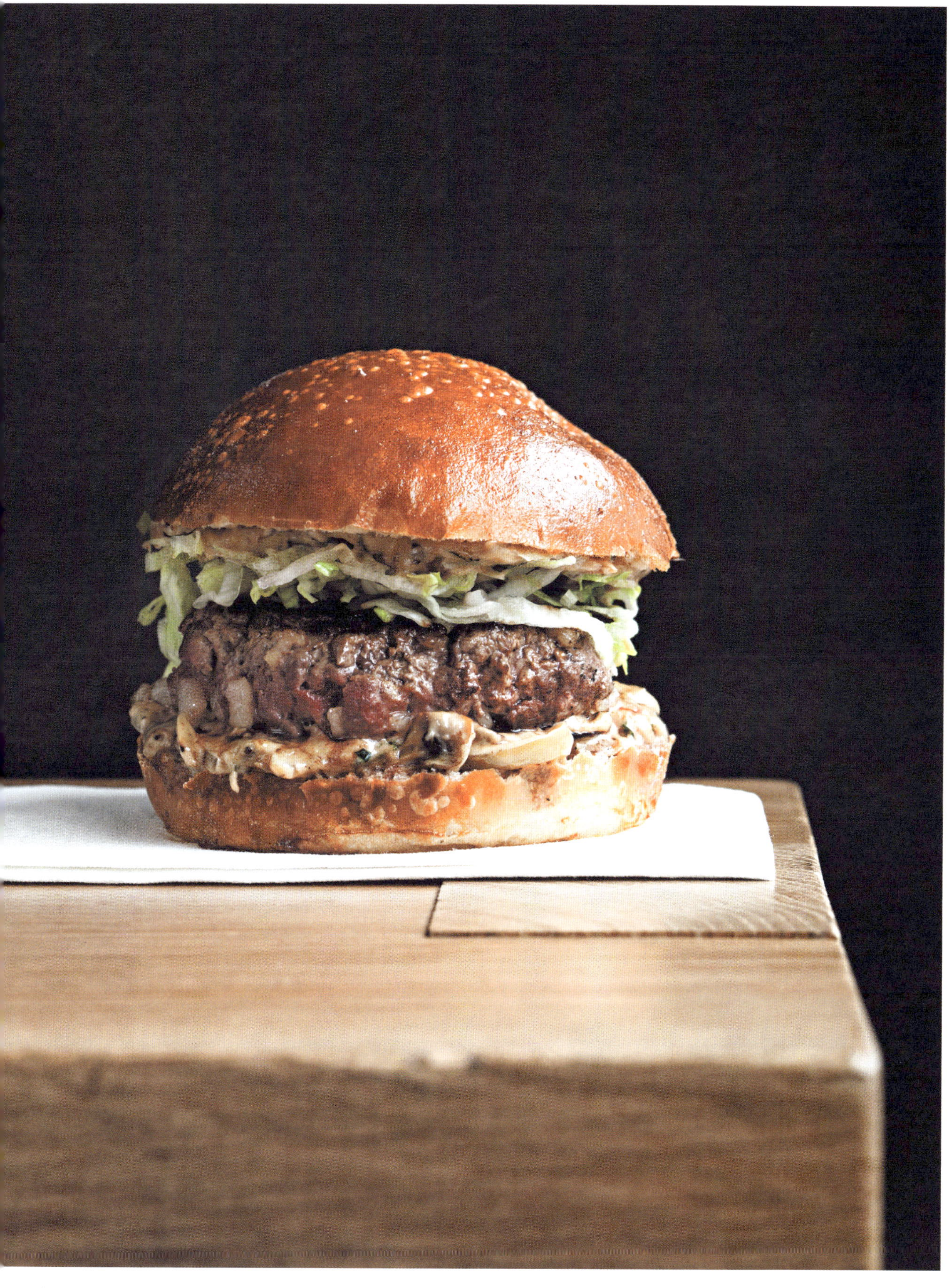

RECIPE NO. 9

LARDO
BEEF, COLONNATA CREAM

Level of difficulty:
Preparation time: 30 mins
Number of hamburgers: 4

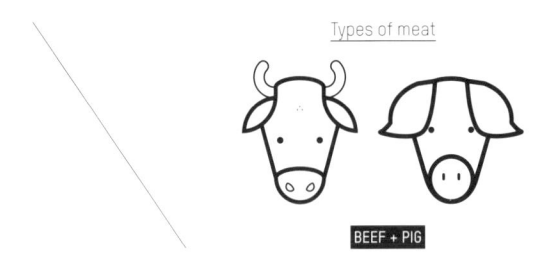

Types of meat

BEEF + PIG

BUNS
| homemade or bought buns | 4 |

PATTIES
| beef, minced (ground) | 500 g (1 lb 2 oz) |
| sea salt | a few pinches |

SAUCE
lardo di Colonnata, cut into small cubes	150 g (5½ oz)
thin (pouring) cream	150 ml (5 fl oz)
thickened beef stock	1 tablespoon
salt	1 pinch
pepper	1 pinch

TOPPINGS
| rocket (arugula) | a large handful |

BUNS
Make the buns as described on page 14 or use ready-made buns.

PATTIES
Form 4 patties from the minced beef and season them with the sea salt.

SAUCE
Sauté the cubes of the lardo gently in a frying pan to render some of the fat. Drain the fat rendered by the lardo, add the cream and stock and allow to reduce, about 10 minutes. Adjust the seasoning if necessary.

COOKING THE PATTIES
Cook the patties in a hot frying pan over high heat, 3 minutes per side for rare patties.

ASSEMBLY
Cut the buns in half horizontally and toast them for 2 minutes under the grill (broiler). Spread the cut side of the bun heels and crowns with the sauce. On the heels put the patties and a small handful of rocket leaves. Top with the crowns.

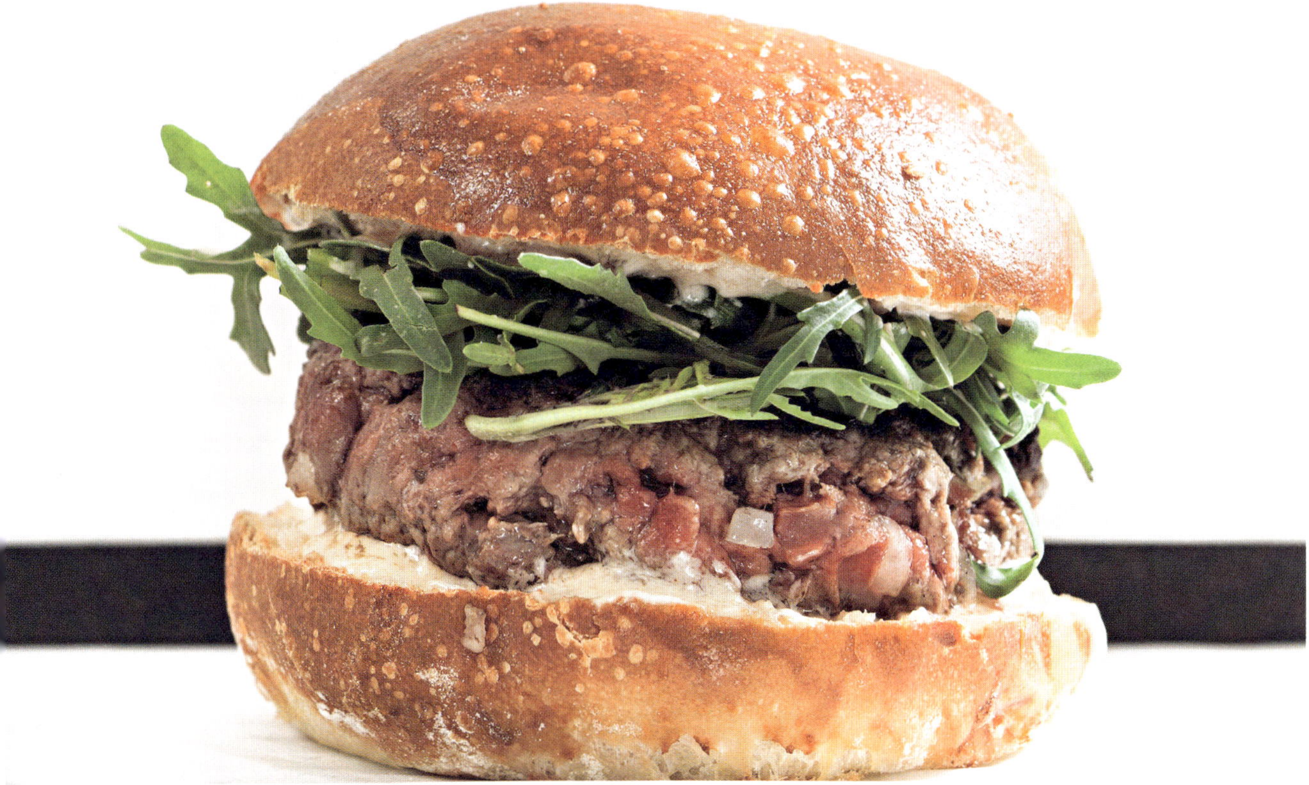

RECIPE NO. 10

SIMPLE
BEEF, FENNEL, PINE NUTS

Level of difficulty:
Preparation time: 40 mins
Number of hamburgers: 4

Type of meat

BEEF

BUNS
homemade or bought buns	4

PATTIES
beef, minced (ground)	500 g (1 lb 2 oz)
sea salt	a few pinches

RELISH
onion, diced	½
garlic, diced	1 clove
olive oil	1 drizzle
fresh ginger, peeled and chopped	30 g (1 oz)
tomatoes	6
salt	1 pinch
pepper	1 pinch

TOPPINGS
pine nuts	2 teaspoons
fennel bulbs	2
semi-dried tomatoes, coarsely chopped	30 g (1 oz)

BUNS
Make the buns as described on page 14 or use ready-made buns.

PATTIES
Form 4 patties from the minced beef and season them with the sea salt.

RELISH
Sauté the onion and garlic in a frying pan over high heat with a little olive oil. Allow to lightly brown, about 8 minutes. Reduce the heat to medium then add the ginger and tomatoes cut into large dice. Let the mixture cook for about 30 minutes, or until broken down, adding water as necessary. Season.

TOPPINGS
While cooking the relish, toast the pine nuts in a frying pan over medium heat for about 2-3 minutes. Remove the tough outer layer of the fennel bulbs and slice the flesh thinly.

COOKING THE PATTIES
Cook the patties in a hot frying pan over high heat, 3 minutes per side for rare patties.

ASSEMBLY
Cut the buns in half horizontally and toast them for 2 minutes under the grill (broiler). Spread the cut side of the bun heels and crowns with the relish. Sprinkle the pine nuts on the heels, and then top with the chopped semi-dried tomatoes, the patties and the slices of fennel. Top with the crowns.

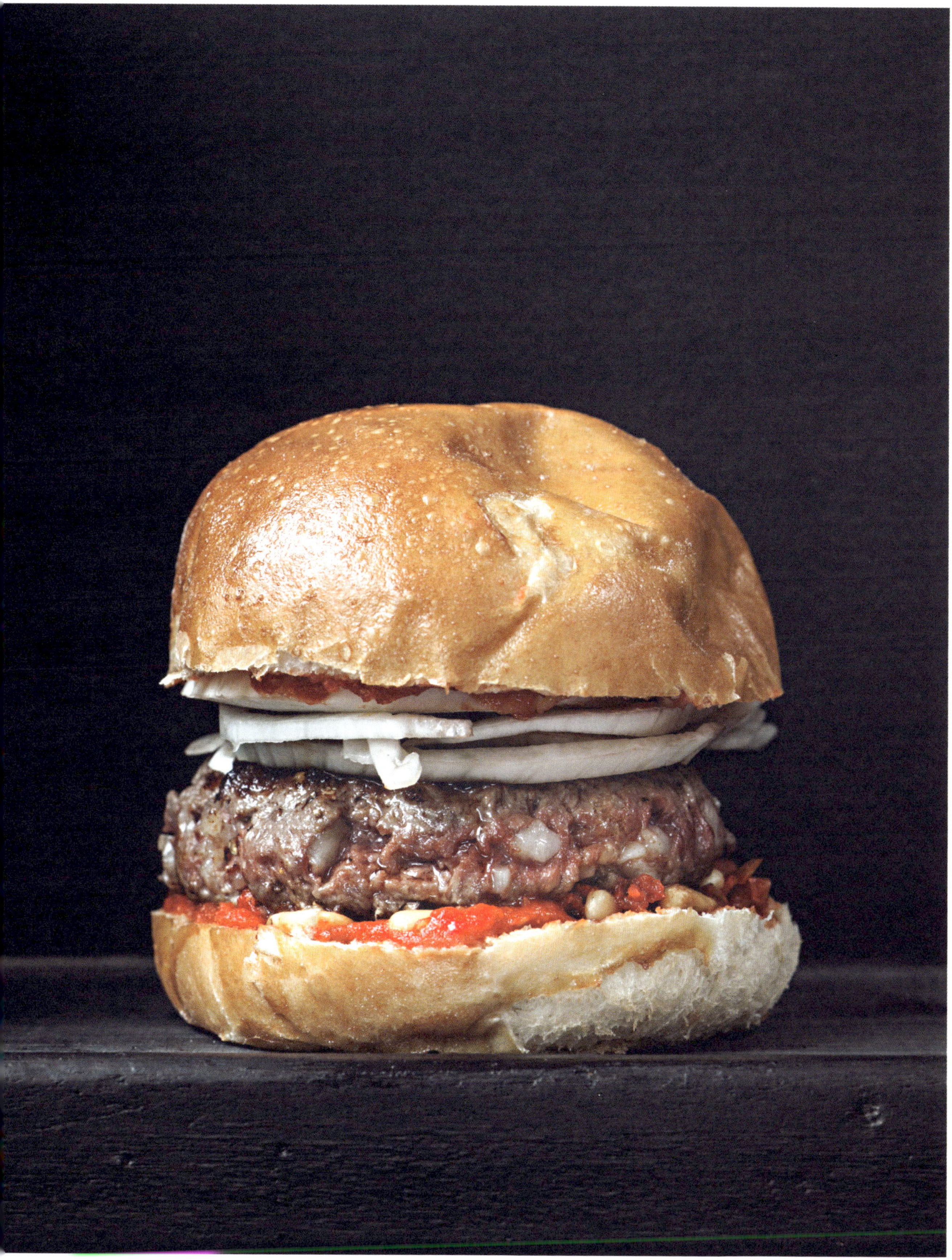

RECIPE NO. 11

SUN
BEEF, GOAT'S CHEESE, EGGPLANT

Level of difficulty:
Preparation time: 40 mins
Number of hamburgers: 4

Type of meat

BEEF

BUNS
homemade or bought buns ... 4

PATTIES
beef, minced (ground) ... **500 g (1 lb 2 oz)**
sea salt ... **a few pinches**

RELISH
eggplant (aubergine), thinly sliced ... **1**
garlic, crushed ... **1 clove**
tomato ... **1**
olive oil ... **1–2 tablespoons**

TOPPINGS
fresh goat's cheese, cut into 4 slices ... **120 g (4¼ oz)**
rocket (arugula) ... **a large handful**

BUNS
Make the buns as described on page 14 or use ready-made buns.

PATTIES
Form 4 patties from the minced beef and season them with the sea salt.

RELISH
Sauté the eggplant, garlic and tomato in olive oil and cook them down into a stew. This will take between 20 and 25 minutes. Season well with sea salt and pepper.

COOKING THE PATTIES
Cook the patties in a hot frying pan over high heat. After 3 minutes of cooking, turn them, put 1 slice of goat's cheese on each, cover with a stainless steel bowl and cook for another 3 minutes.

ASSEMBLY
Cut the buns in half horizontally and toast them for 2 minutes under the grill (broiler). Spread the cut side of the bun heels with half of the eggplant–tomato relish, add the patties with the melted goat's cheese, then a few rocket leaves and the remaining relish. Top with the crowns.

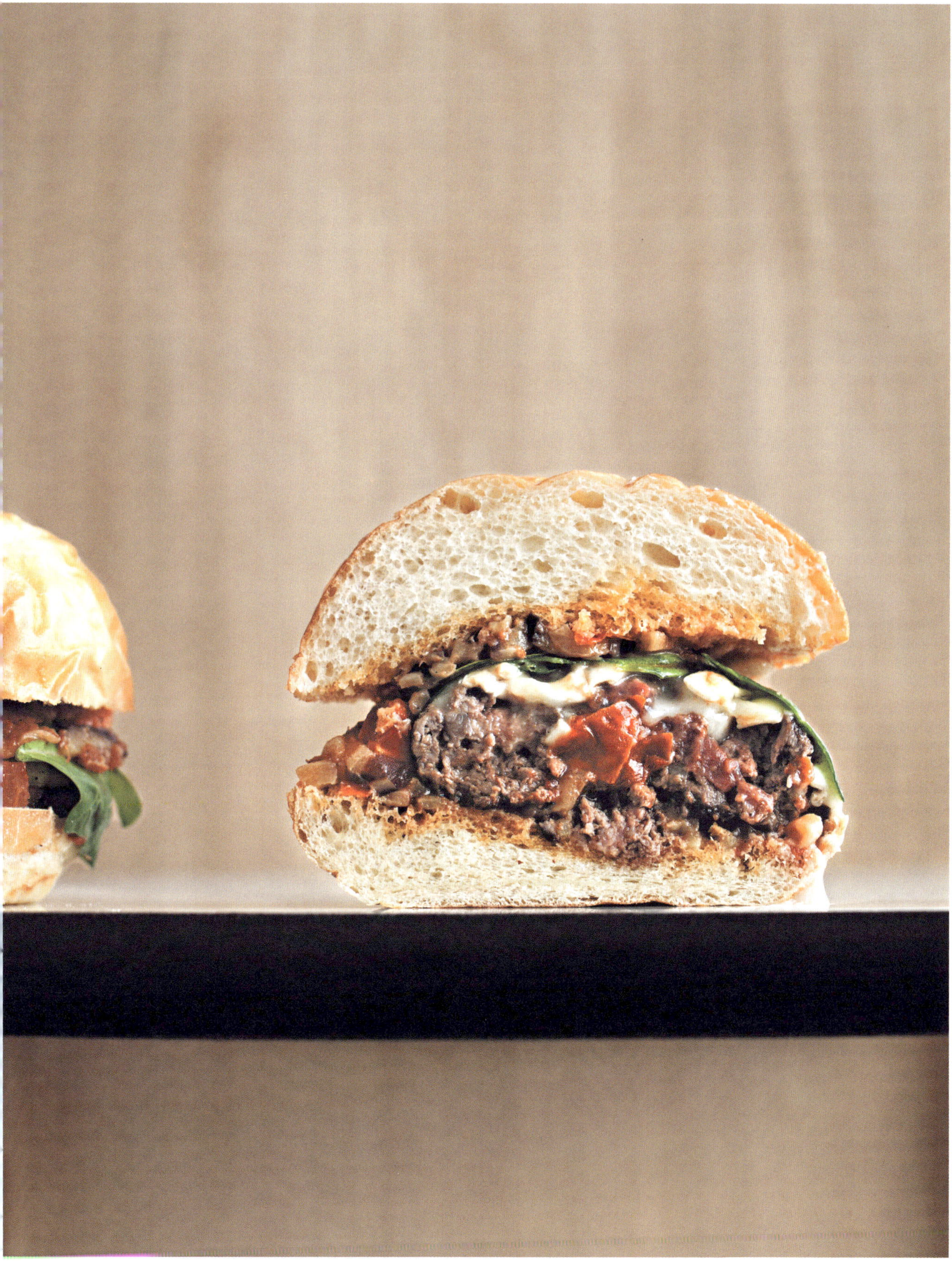

RECIPE NO. 12

WINE
BEEF, WINE REDUCTION

Level of difficulty: 🍔🍔
Preparation time: 40 mins
Number of hamburgers: 4

Type of meat

BEEF

BUNS
homemade or bought buns 4

WINE REDUCTION
French shallots, finely chopped 2
butter .... **1 knob**
red wine .... **500 ml (17 fl oz/2 cups)**
sugar .... **150 g (5½ oz)**

PATTIES
beef, minced (ground) .... **500 g (1 lb 2 oz)**

TOPPINGS
rocket (arugula) .... **a large handful**

BUNS
Make the buns as described on page 14 or use ready-made buns.

WINE REDUCTION
Sauté the shallots in the butter in a heavy based frying pan for 10 minutes until they are golden brown. Pour in the wine and reduce by half. Add the sugar and reduce to about 170 ml (5½ fl oz/⅔ cup) then pour into a bowl. Allow to cool.

PATTIES
Form 4 patties from the minced beef and before cooking them, put them in the bowl of wine reduction to coat.

COOKING THE PATTIES
Cook the patties in a hot frying pan over high heat, 3 minutes per side for rare patties. During cooking, pour 1 tablespoon of the wine reduction on them, on both sides. Reserve some of the reduction for the assembly stage.

ASSEMBLY
Cut the buns in half horizontally and toast them for 2 minutes under the grill (broiler). On the cut side of the bun heels put the patties, remaining wine reduction and rocket. Top with the crowns.

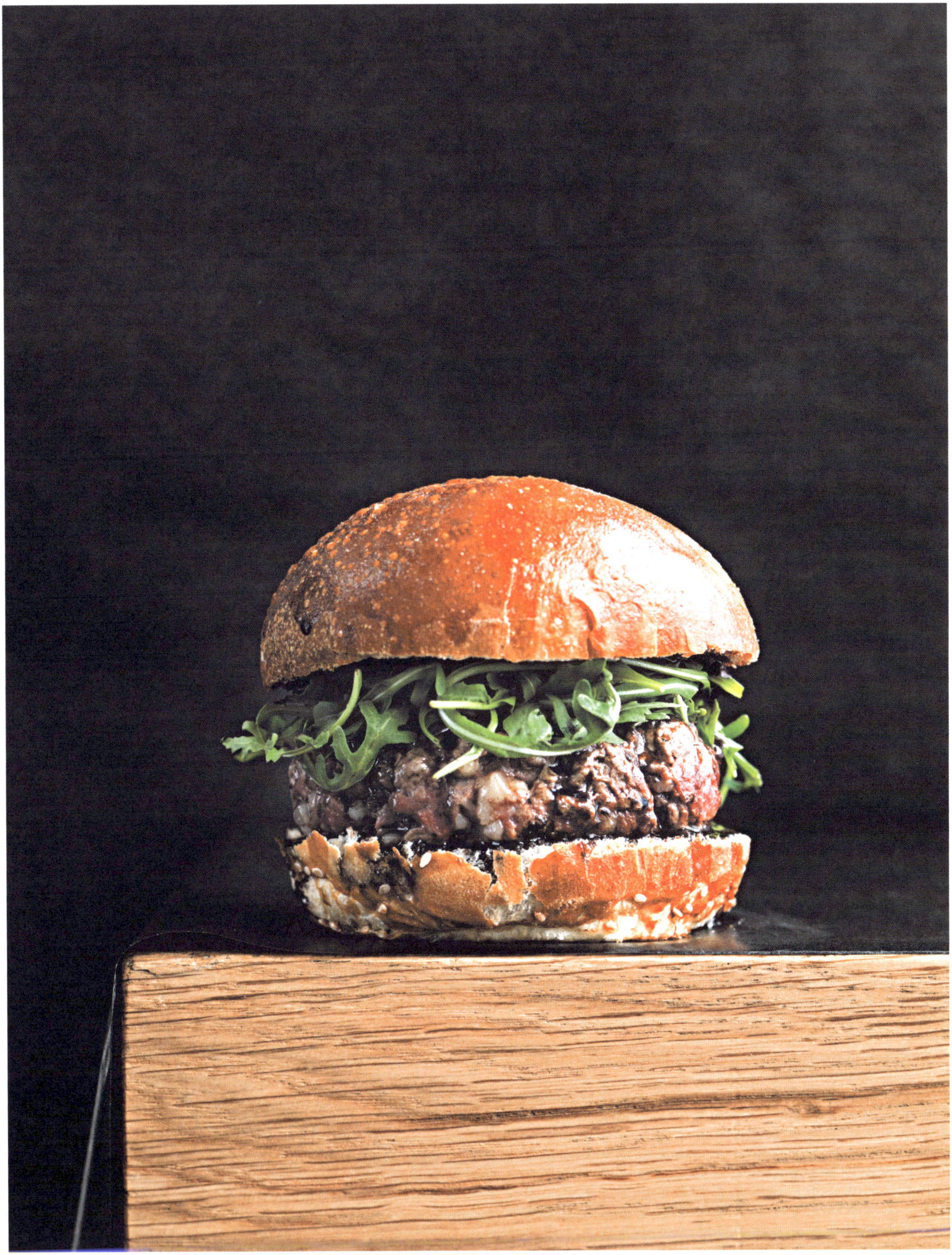

RECIPE NO. 13

BEET
BEEF, BEETROOT, WASABI

Level of difficulty:
Preparation time: 20 mins
Number of hamburgers: 4

Type of meat

BEEF

BUNS
homemade or bought buns	4

PATTIES
beef, minced (ground)	500 g (1 lb 2 oz)
sea salt	a few pinches

TOPPINGS
beetroot (beet), cooked	1 large, about 230 g (8½ oz)
spring onion (scallion), chopped	1
parsley, chopped	a few leaves
salt	1 pinch
pepper	1 pinch
wasabi	about 1 teaspoon
olive oil	1 drizzle
rocket (arugula)	a few leaves

BUNS
Make the buns as described on page 14 or use ready-made buns.

PATTIES
Form 4 patties from the minced beef and season them with the sea salt.

TOPPINGS
Cut the beetroot into matchsticks. Combine the beetroot with the spring onion and parsley and season with salt and pepper. Add the wasabi with a drop of olive oil and mix together.

COOKING THE PATTIES
Cook the patties in a hot frying pan over high heat, 3 minutes per side for rare patties.

ASSEMBLY
Cut the buns in half horizontally and toast them for 2 minutes under the grill (broiler). On the cut side of the bun heels add a layer of the beetroot-parsley-wasabi mixture, the patties, then another layer of the beetroot-parsley-wasabi mixture. Top with rocket and the crowns.

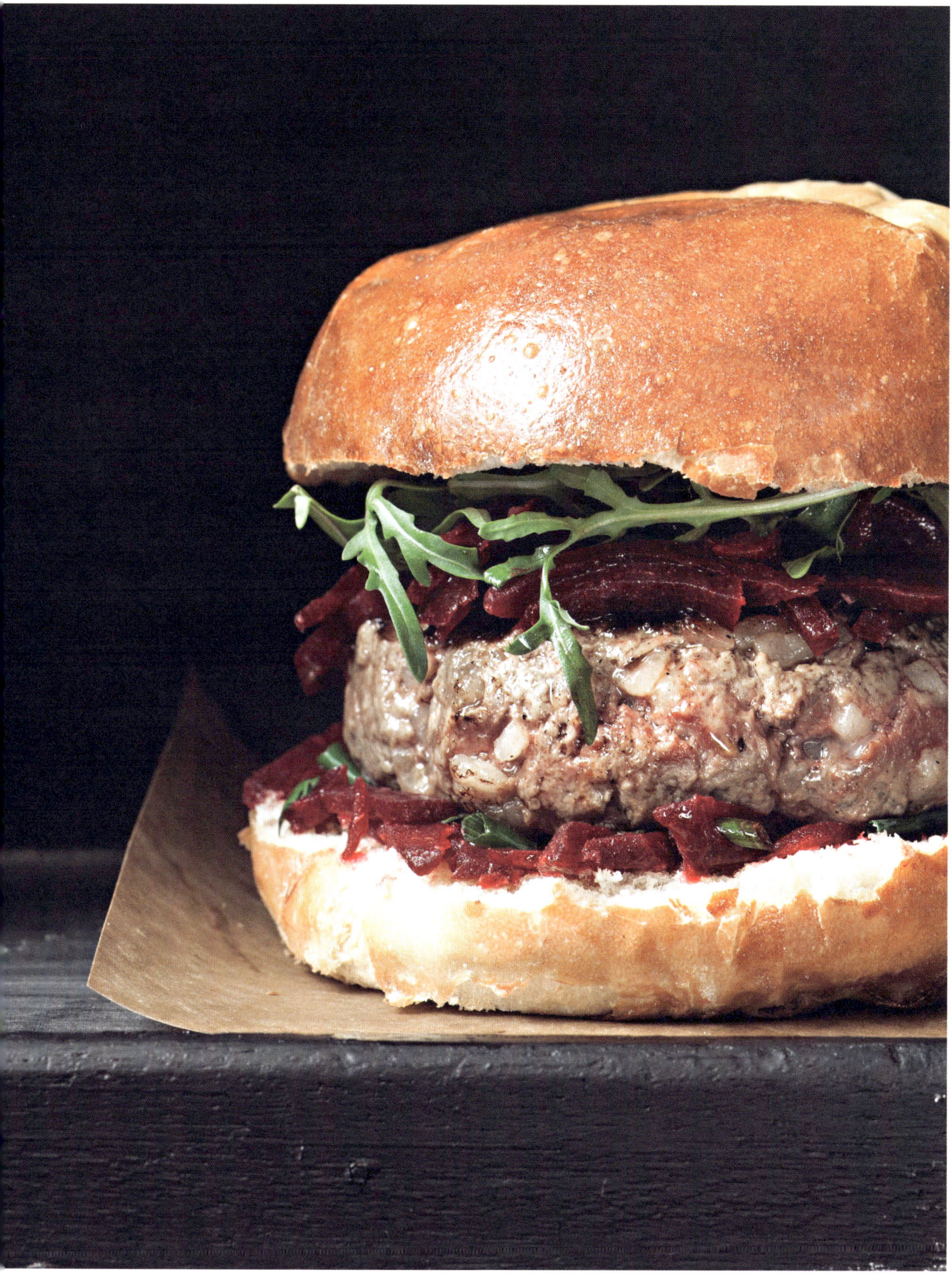

RECIPE NO. 14

CHICK
THE CLASSIC WITH CHICKEN

Level of difficulty:
Preparation time: 30 mins
Number of hamburgers: 4

Type of meat

CHICKEN

BUNS
homemade or bought buns	4

PATTIES
chicken breast fillet	**500 g (1 lb 2 oz)**
sea salt	**a few pinches**
olive oil	**a drizzle**

SAUCE
onion, thinly sliced	1
olive oil	1 drizzle
crème fraîche	200 g (7 oz)
parsley, chopped	75 g (2¾ oz)

TOPPINGS
baby spinach	70 g (2½ oz/1½ cups)

BUNS
Make the buns as described on page 14 or use ready-made buns.

PATTIES
Dice the chicken into small pieces and form into 4 patties, pressing them together well. Set aside in the refrigerator until ready to use.

SAUCE
Brown the onion in a frying pan over high heat with the olive oil. Set a quarter aside. Put the frying pan over low heat and add the crème fraîche and parsley. Cook, stirring until the mixture reduces. Season with sea salt and freshly ground black pepper.

COOKING THE PATTIES
Season the patties with the sea salt. Cook the patties in a hot frying pan over high heat with the olive oil for 5 minutes on each side.

ASSEMBLY
Cut the buns in half horizontally and toast them for 2 minutes under the grill (broiler). Spread the cut side of the heels and crowns with the sauce. Put the chicken patties on the heels, then top with the reserved onions and the spinach. Finish with the crowns.

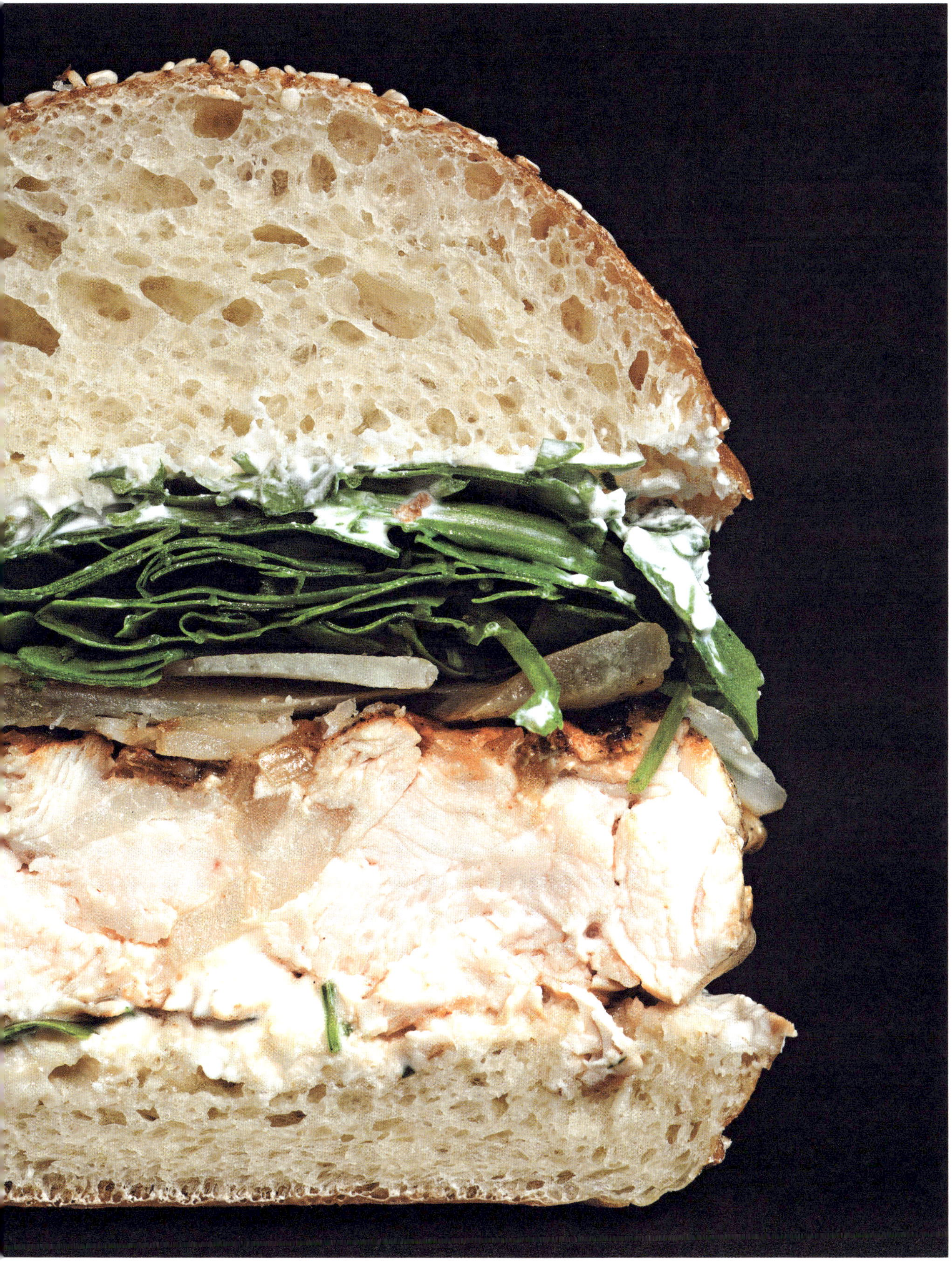

RECIPE NO. 15

BASQUE
BASQUE-STYLE CHICKEN

Level of difficulty:
Preparation time: 30 mins
Number of hamburgers: 4

Type of meat

CHICKEN

BUNS
homemade or bought buns — 4

PATTIES
chicken breast fillet — **500 g (1 lb 2 oz)**
sea salt — **a few pinches**
olive oil — **1 drizzle**

RELISH
red capsicums (peppers), seeded, membranes removed and sliced into thin strips — **2**
tomatoes, diced — **2**
onion, diced — **1**
olive oil — **100 ml (3½ fl oz)**
Espelette chilli powder — **1 teaspoon**

TOPPINGS
rocket (arugula) — **a large handful**

BUNS
Make the buns as described on page 14 or use ready-made buns.

PATTIES
Dice the chicken into small pieces and form into 4 patties, pressing them together well. Set aside in the refrigerator until ready to use.

RELISH
In a saucepan, stew the vegetables with the olive oil and chilli powder for 15 minutes over low heat.

COOKING THE PATTIES
Season the patties with the sea salt. Cook the patties in a hot frying pan over high heat with the olive oil for 5 minutes on each side.

ASSEMBLY
Cut the buns in half horizontally and toast them for 2 minutes under the grill (broiler). Top the cut side of the bun heels with half the capsicum-tomato-onion relish, add the patties, then the remaining relish and the rocket. Top with the crowns.

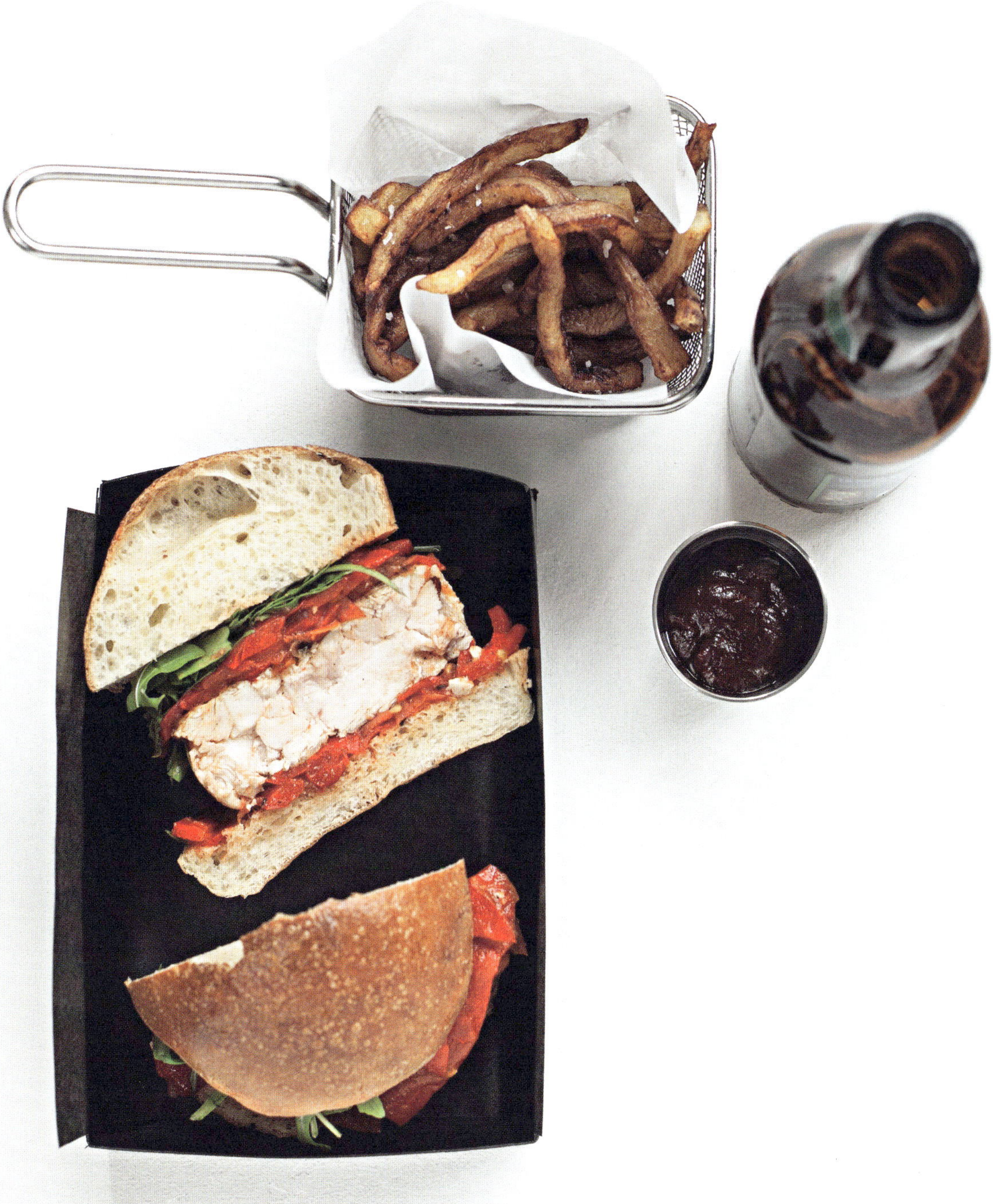

RECIPE NO. 16

COCO
CHICKEN, COCONUT

Level of difficulty: 🍔🍔
Preparation time: 30 mins + 40 mins refrigeration time
Number of hamburgers: 4

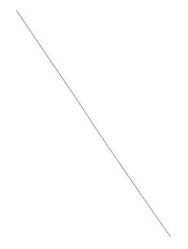

Type of meat

CHICKEN

BUNS
homemade or bought buns	4

PATTIES
chicken breast fillet	**500 g (1 lb 2 oz)**
sea salt	**a few pinches**
olive oil	**1 drizzle**

COCONUT DISCS
coconut cream	**250 ml (9 fl oz/1 cup)**
agar-agar	**1 tablespoon**

RELISH
onions, diced	**2**
olive oil	**1 drizzle**

TOPPINGS
rocket (arugula)	**a large handful**

BUNS
Make the buns as described on page 14 or use ready-made buns.

PATTIES
Dice the chicken into small pieces and form into 4 patties, pressing them together well. Set aside in the refrigerator until ready to use.

COCONUT DISCS
Boil the coconut cream in a saucepan for about 5 minutes. Add the agar-agar and stir for 5 minutes. Remove from the heat. Put a 250 ml (9 fl oz/1 cup) capacity mould, roughly the same diameter as a hamburger patty, on a dish or tray and pour in the mixture. Refrigerate for 40 minutes. When ready to use, remove from the mould and cut the disc into four horizontally so you have 4 rounds.

RELISH
Meanwhile, sauté the onion in a saucepan with the olive oil over low heat and stew for about 15–20 minutes until caramelised.

COOKING THE PATTIES
Season the patties with the sea salt and cook in a hot frying pan over medium-high heat with the olive oil, 5 minutes per side.

ASSEMBLY
Cut the buns in half horizontally and toast them for 2 minutes under the grill (broiler). Top the cut side of the bun heels with the onion relish, add the chicken patties, then the coconut discs and the rocket. Top with the crowns.

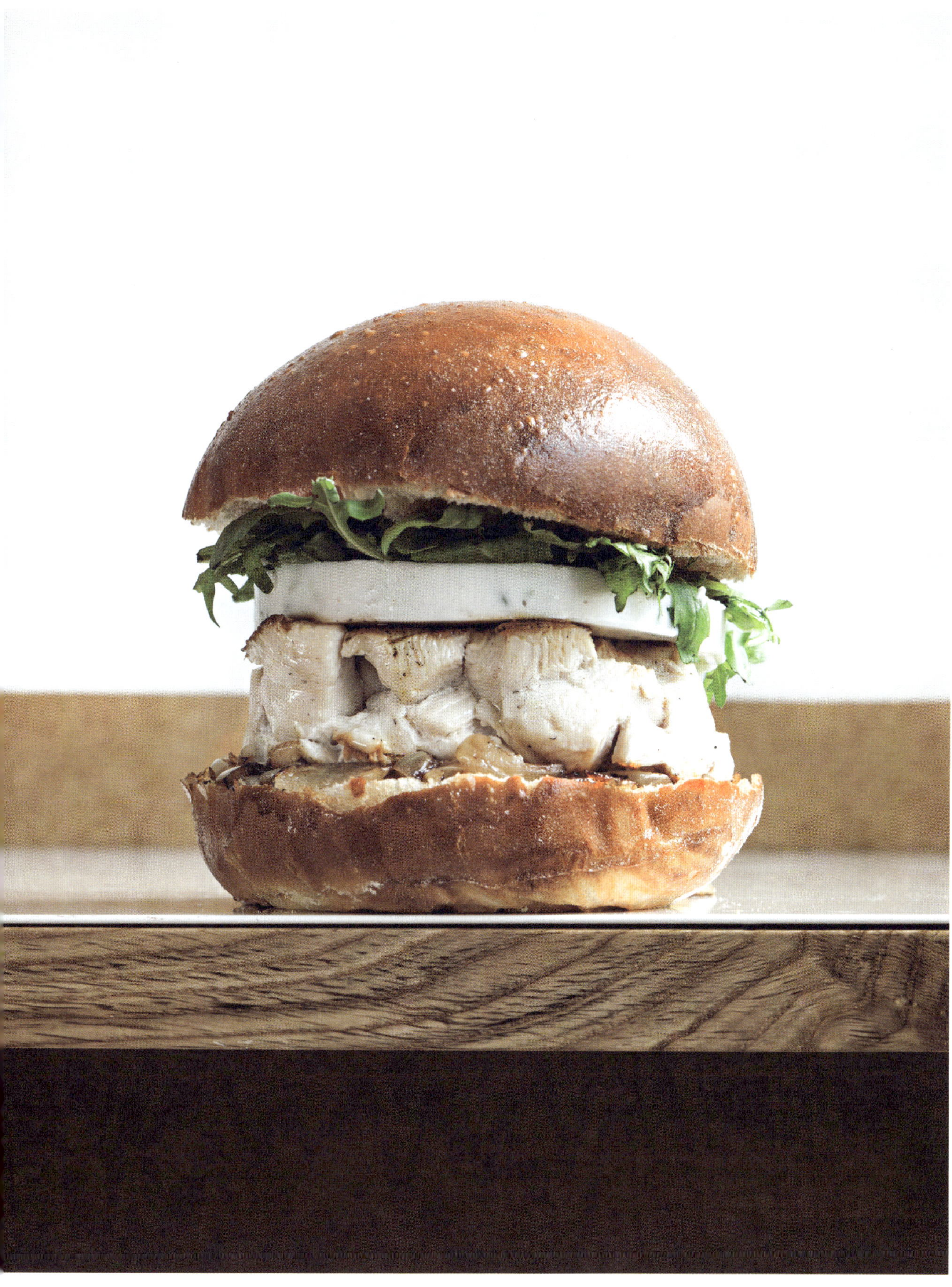

RECIPE NO. 17
RED
SPICED CHICKEN, BEETROOT

Level of difficulty:
Preparation time: 30 mins
Number of hamburgers: 4

Type of meat: CHICKEN

BUNS
homemade or bought buns	4

PATTIES
chicken breast fillet	500 g (1 lb 2 oz)
sea salt	a few pinches
olive oil	1 drizzle

BEETROOT MIX
beetroot (beets), cooked	2
garlic, chopped	2 cloves
orange juice, fresh	2 tablespoons
lime juice, fresh	1 tablespoon

SAUCE
ras el-hanout spice mix	1 pinch
parsley, chopped	75 g (2¾ oz)
Greek-style yoghurt	200 g (7 oz/¾ cup)

TOPPINGS
baby spinach	45 g (1¾ oz/1 cup)

BUNS
Make the buns as described on page 14 or use ready-made buns.

PATTIES
Dice the chicken into small pieces and form into 4 patties, pressing them together well. Set aside in the refrigerator until ready to use.

BEETROOT MIX
Cut the beetroot into strips, combine with the garlic and orange and lime juices. Set aside in the refrigerator.

SAUCE
Combine the ras el-hanout and parsley with the Greek yoghurt.

COOKING THE PATTIES
Season the patties with the sea salt. Heat a little olive oil in a frying pan over high heat. Brown the patties for 5 minutes on each side.

ASSEMBLY
Cut the buns in half horizontally and toast them for 2 minutes under the grill (broiler). Spread the cut side of the bun heels and crowns with the yoghurt sauce. On the heels add half the beetroot mix, the patties and some spinach, then finish with the remaining beetroot mix. Top with the crowns.

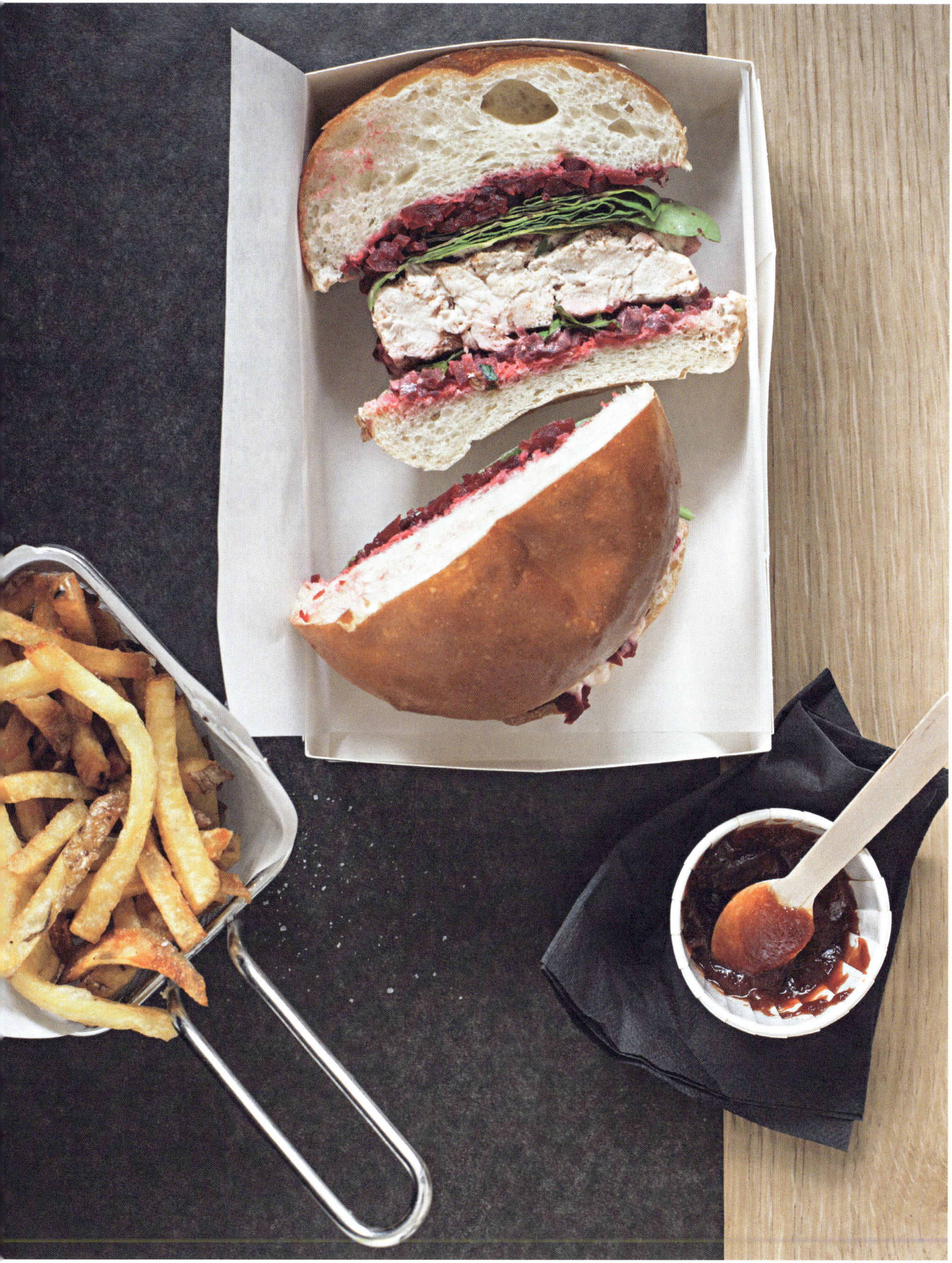

RECIPE NO. 18

QUINCE
CHICKEN, QUINCE JAM

Level of difficulty:
Preparation time: 1 hour (less if using ready-made quince jam)
Number of hamburgers: 4

Type of meat

CHICKEN

BUNS
homemade or bought buns 4

PATTIES
chicken breast fillet .... 500 g (1 lb 2 oz)
sea salt .... a few pinches
olive oil .... 1 drizzle

QUINCE JAM
quinces .... 400 g (14 oz)
sugar .... 150 g (5½ oz)
water .... 250 ml (9 fl oz/1 cup)
Gorgonzola cheese .... 80 g (2¾ oz)

RELISH
French shallots, thinly sliced 2
pickled marinated ginger, chopped
.... 40 g (1½ oz)
olive oil .... 1 drizzle
Madras curry powder .... 2 teaspoons

TOPPINGS
rocket (arugula) .... a large handful

BUNS
Make the buns as described on page 14 or use ready-made buns.

PATTIES
Dice the chicken into small pieces and form into 4 patties, pressing them together well. Set aside in the refrigerator until ready to use.

QUINCE JAM
Peel, core and coarsely chop the quinces. Put them in a large saucepan with the sugar and water. Cook for about 40 minutes, or until thick and jammy, over medium heat, stirring occasionally. Cut the Gorgonzola into small cubes, then mix them with the quince jam.

RELISH
In a frying pan, sauté the shallots and ginger over medium heat for about 10 minutes with the olive oil and curry powder until the mixture begins to brown.

COOKING THE PATTIES
Season the patties with the sea salt. Heat a frying pan over high heat. Brown the patties for 5 minutes on each side.

ASSEMBLY
Cut the buns in half horizontally and toast them for 2 minutes under the grill (broiler). Spread the quince jam with Gorgonzola on the cut side of the bun heels, then the shallot-ginger relish. Add the patties and a few rocket leaves. Finish with the crowns.

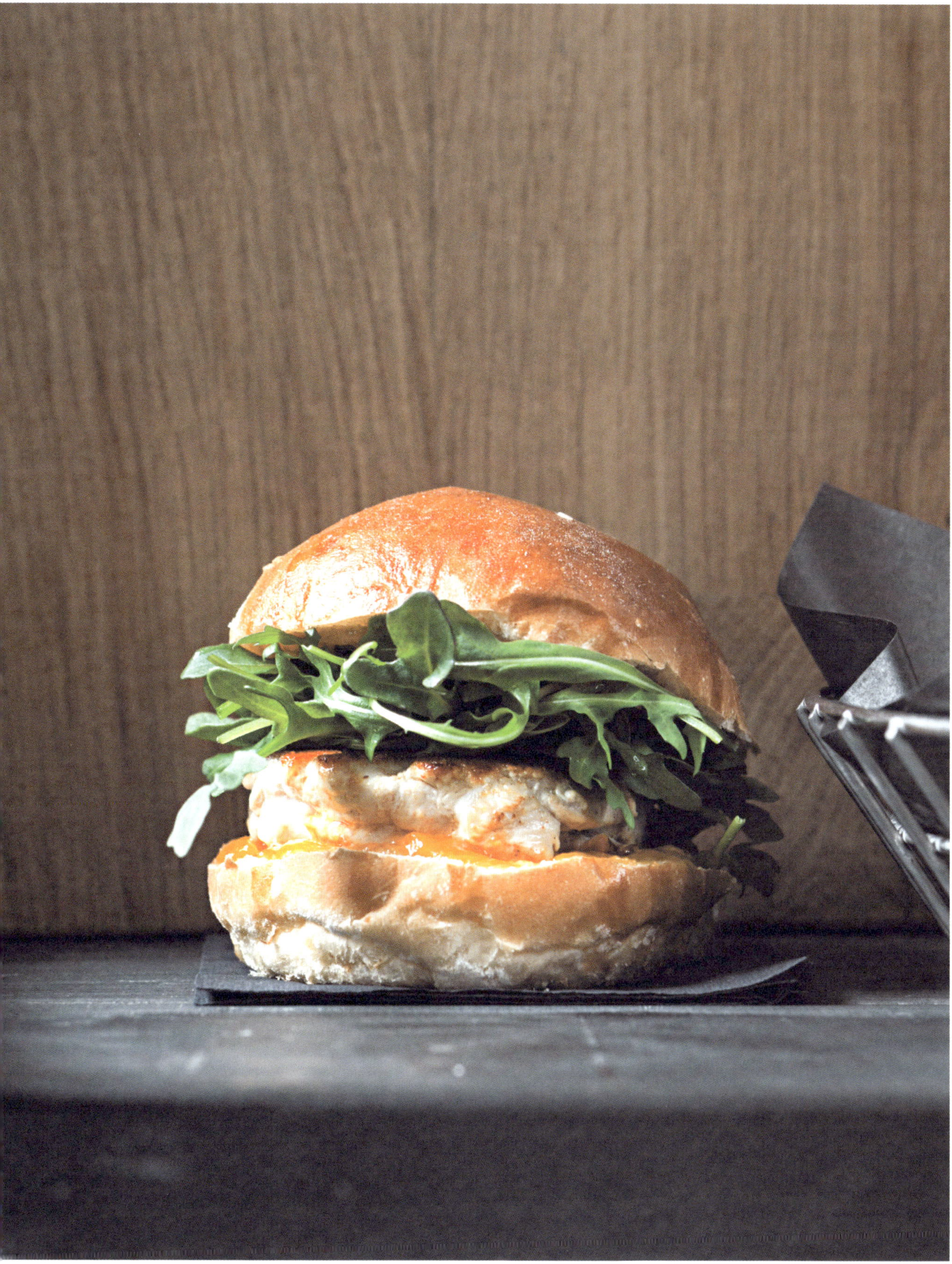

RECIPE NO. 19

HERBS
THE CLASSIC WITH LAMB

Level of difficulty:
Preparation time: 1 hour
Number of hamburgers: 4

Type of meat

LAMB

BUNS
homemade or bought buns	4

PATTIES
lamb, minced (ground)	500 g (1 lb 2 oz)
sea salt	a few pinches

SAUCE
lamb bones from the butcher	100 g (3½ oz)
carrot, chopped	1
onion, chopped	1
celery, chopped	½ stalk
thyme leaves	4 tablespoons
dried bay leaves	a few

TOPPINGS
onion, thinly sliced	1
olive oil	1 drizzle
baby spinach	70 g (2½ oz/1½ cups)

BUNS
Make the buns as described on page 14 or use ready-made buns.

PATTIES
Form 4 patties from the minced lamb and season them with the sea salt.

SAUCE
Brown the lamb bones in a frying pan, add the vegetables, let them brown, then pour over 1 litre (35 fl oz/4 cups) of water to just cover. Add the thyme and bay leaves and reduce for about 40 minutes. Strain and discard the solids. Return the liquid to the pan and continue reducing until you have a thick dark liquid. (Similar preparations are available in supermarkets if you want to skip this step.)

TOPPINGS
Brown the onion in olive oil in a frying pan at the same time as the patties for about 4 minutes.

COOKING THE PATTIES
Cook the patties in a hot frying pan over high heat, 4 minutes per side.

ASSEMBLY
Cut the buns in half horizontally and toast them for 2 minutes under the grill (broiler). Spread the cut side of the heels and crowns with the sauce and then on top of the heels put the onion, patties and spinach. Top with the crowns.

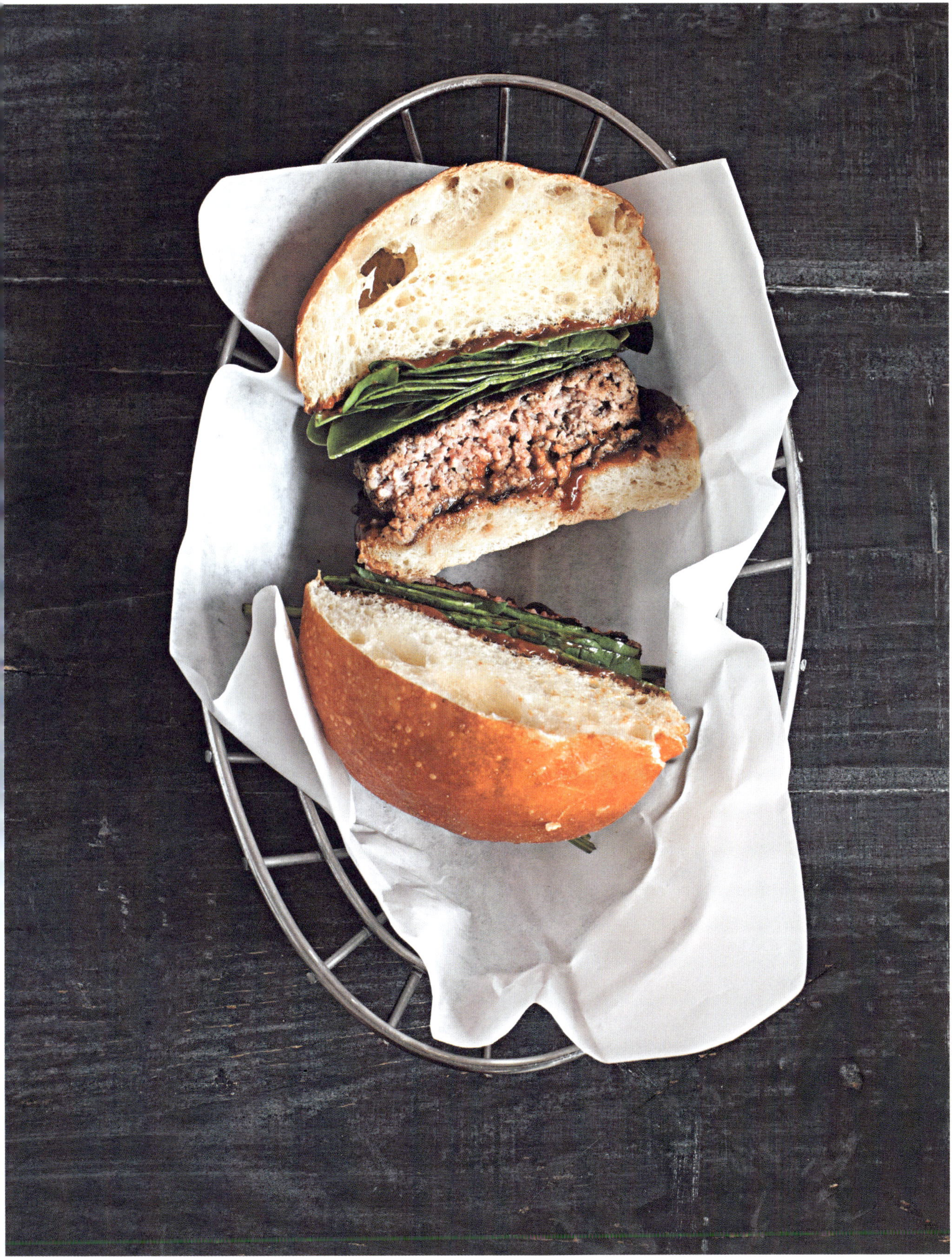

RECIPE NO. 20

SWEET
THE CLASSIC WITH VEAL

Level of difficulty: ●●
Preparation time: 30 mins
Number of hamburgers: 4

Type of meat

VEAL

BUNS
homemade or bought buns — 4

PATTIES
veal, minced (ground) — 500 g (1 lb 2 oz)
sea salt — a few pinches

PARMESAN TUILES
parmesan cheese, finely grated — 50 g (1¾ oz/⅓ cup)

RELISH
carrots — 2
green capsicum (pepper) — ½
red capsicum (pepper) — ½
olive oil — 100 ml (3½ fl oz)
fresh mint, chopped — 2 teaspoons
sweet chilli sauce — 30 ml (1 fl oz)

TOPPINGS
rocket (arugula) — a large handful

BUNS
Make the buns as described on page 14 or use ready-made buns.

PATTIES
Form 4 patties from the minced veal and put them in the refrigerator while preparing the relish.

PARMESAN TUILES
Preheat the oven to 190°C (375°F/Gas 5). Make 4 rounds of parmesan on a greased baking tray. Put in the oven for 4 minutes, or until just golden. Allow the tuiles to cool then peel them off the tray.

RELISH
Peel and cut the carrots into matchsticks. Remove the seeds and membranes from the capsicums and cut into matchsticks. In a saucepan over medium heat, sauté the carrots and capsicums with the olive oil, and stew for about 20 minutes. Add the chopped mint and sweet chilli sauce (reserve a little to spread on the bun heels during the assembly stage), then remove from the heat.

COOKING THE PATTIES
Season the patties with the sea salt. In a hot frying pan over high heat, cook the patties for 3 minutes on each side.

ASSEMBLY
Cut the buns in half horizontally and toast them for 2 minutes under the grill (broiler). Spread the cut side of the bun heels with the reserved sweet chilli sauce. Add half the carrot-capsicum relish, the patties, the remaining relish, the parmesan tuiles and the rocket. Top with the crowns.

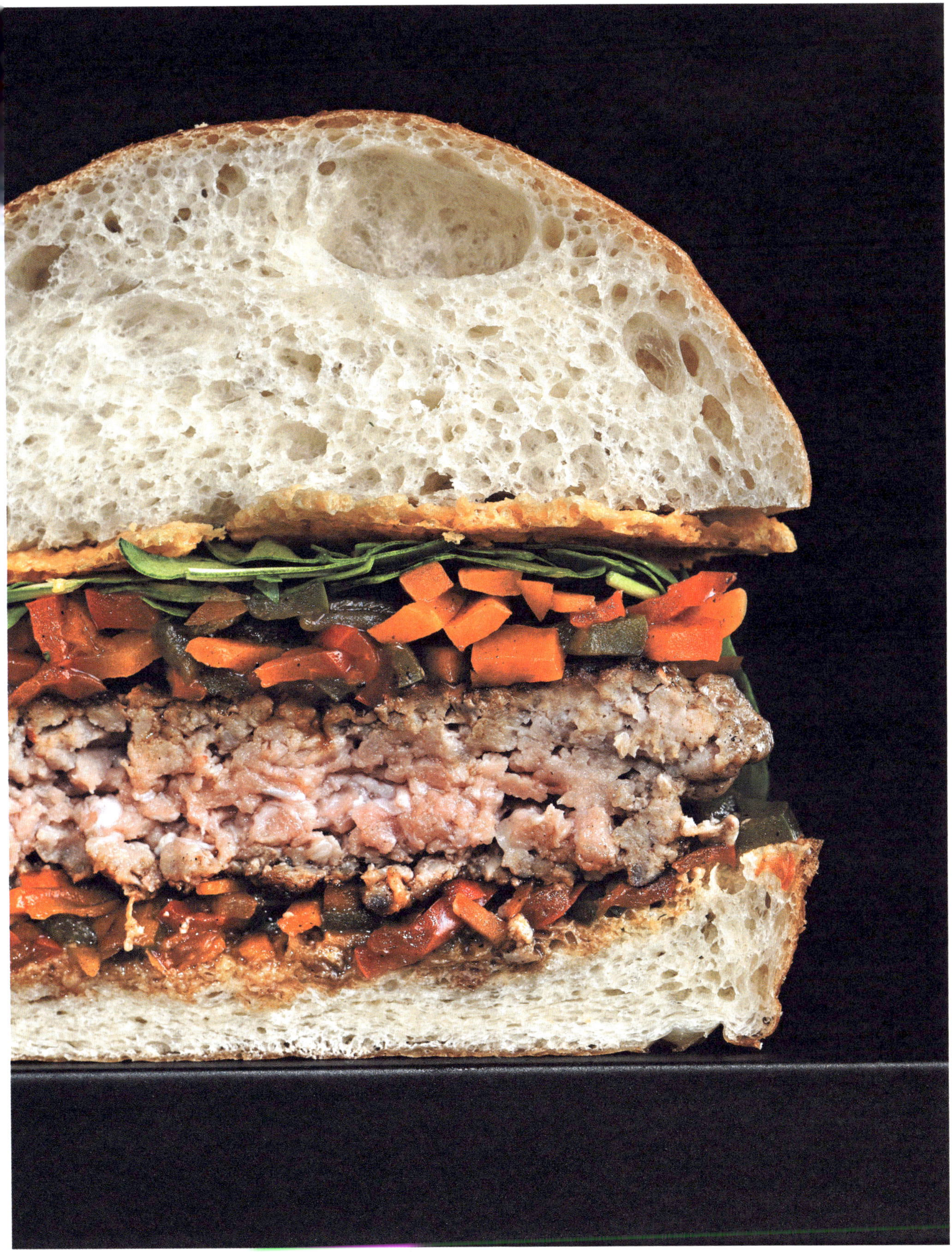

RECIPE NO. 21

FUNGHI
VEAL, WILD MOREL MUSHROOMS

Level of difficulty:
Preparation time: 20 mins + 20 mins soaking time
Number of hamburgers: 4

Type of meat

VEAL

BUNS
homemade or bought buns	4

PATTIES
veal, minced (ground)	**500 g (1 lb 2 oz)**
sea salt	**a few pinches**

RELISH
dried morel mushrooms	**10**
onion, sliced	**1**
olive oil	**1 drizzle**

TOPPINGS
aged Gruyère cheese	**60 g (2¼ oz)**
baby spinach	**45 g (1¾ oz/1 cup)**

BUNS
Make the buns as described on page 14 or use ready-made buns.

PATTIES
Form 4 patties from the minced veal and put them in the refrigerator while preparing the relish.

RELISH
Soak the mushrooms for 20 minutes in a bowl of lukewarm water to rehydrate them. Drain and rinse. Sauté the onion in a frying pan with the mushrooms and olive oil for 7–8 minutes over medium heat.

COOKING THE PATTIES
Season the patties with the sea salt and cook in a hot frying pan over high heat for 3 minutes on one side. Cut the Gruyère cheese into thin slices. Turn the patties over, put the Gruyère on top, cover with a stainless steel bowl or a cloche, and cook for another 3 minutes.

ASSEMBLY
Cut the buns in half horizontally and toast them for 2 minutes under the grill (broiler). Put the patties with the Gruyère on the cut side of the bun heels, add the onion-mushroom relish and a few leaves of spinach. Top with the crowns.

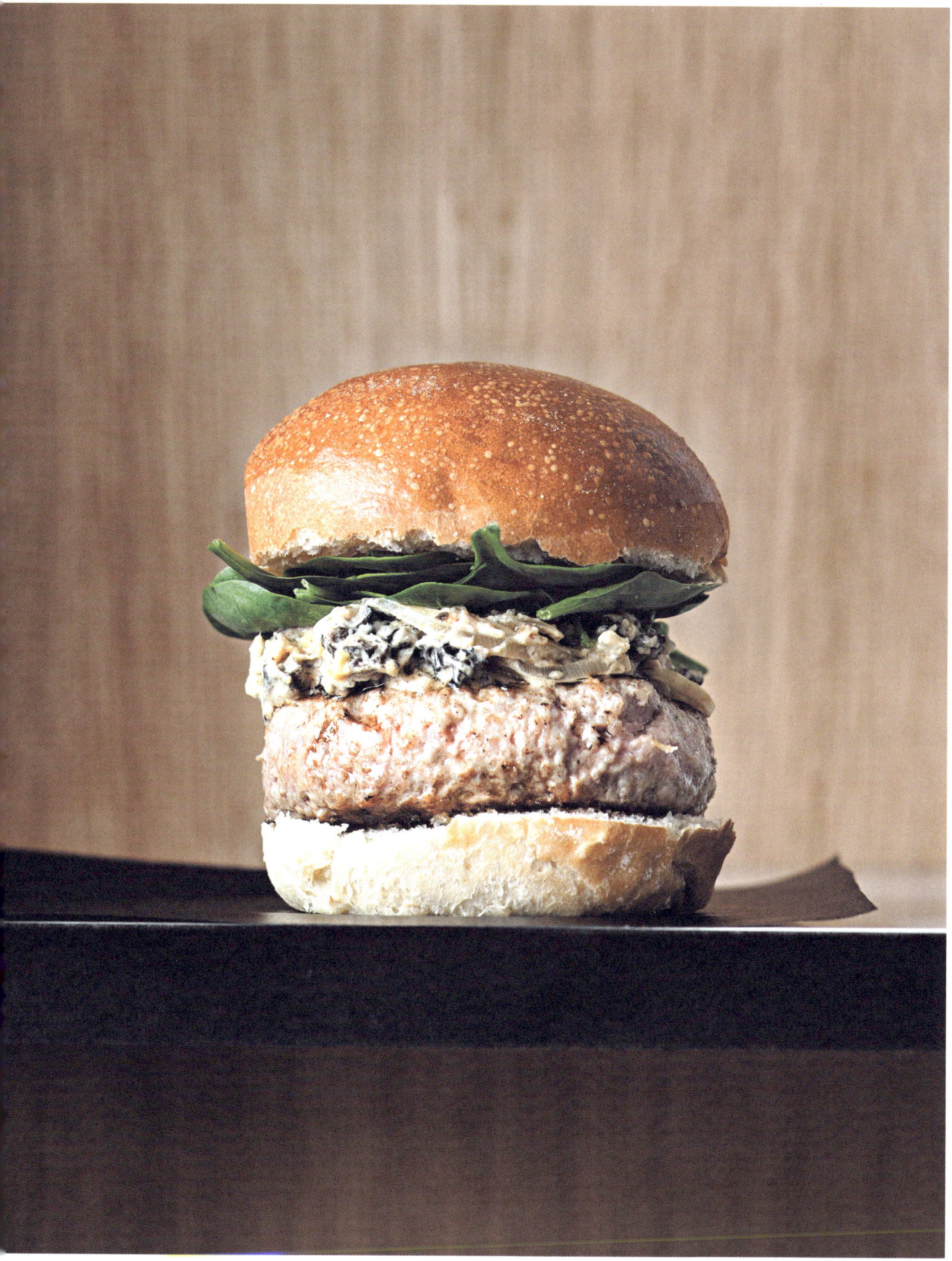

RECIPE NO. 22

MAGRET

DUCK, ROSTI

Level of difficulty:
Preparation time: 40 mins + 1 hour resting time
Number of hamburgers: 4

Type of meat

DUCK

BUNS
| homemade or bought buns | 4 |

PATTIES
duck breast fillet	4
sea salt	a few pinches
olive oil	1 drizzle

ROSTI
potatoes	400 g (14 oz)
onions	2
eggs	3
salt	½ teaspoon
pepper	½ teaspoon
nutmeg	1 pinch
butter	1 knob

TOPPINGS
| barbecue sauce (see page 26) | 2 tablespoons |
| iceberg lettuce, shredded | ¼ |

BUNS
Make the buns as described on page 14 or use ready-made buns.

PATTIES
Remove the fat from the duck breasts by separating the layer of fat from the flesh. To make the patties, use a mincer or cut the meat into cubes, then form the patties by hand, pressing them well so that they hold together during cooking. Season the patties with the sea salt. Set aside in the refrigerator for 10 minutes.

ROSTI
Peel the potatoes and onions. Grate them, then put them in a container and cover with water. Set aside to rest in the refrigerator for 1 hour, covered. Drain the potatoes and onions. Lightly beat the eggs and add them to the mixture with the salt, pepper and nutmeg. Form 4 nicely rounded rösti using a cookie cutter the size of the buns, then cook in a frying pan in the butter over medium heat, for 5 minutes on each side, turning them over several times.

COOKING THE PATTIES
Halfway through cooking the potato rösti, start cooking the patties. Add the olive oil to a hot frying pan over high heat, then add the patties, cooking for 4 minutes per side for pink patties.

ASSEMBLY
Cut the buns in half horizontally and toast them for 2 minutes under the grill (broiler). Spread the cut side of the bun heels with the barbecue sauce, add the patties, the potato rösti and the shredded lettuce. Top with the crowns.

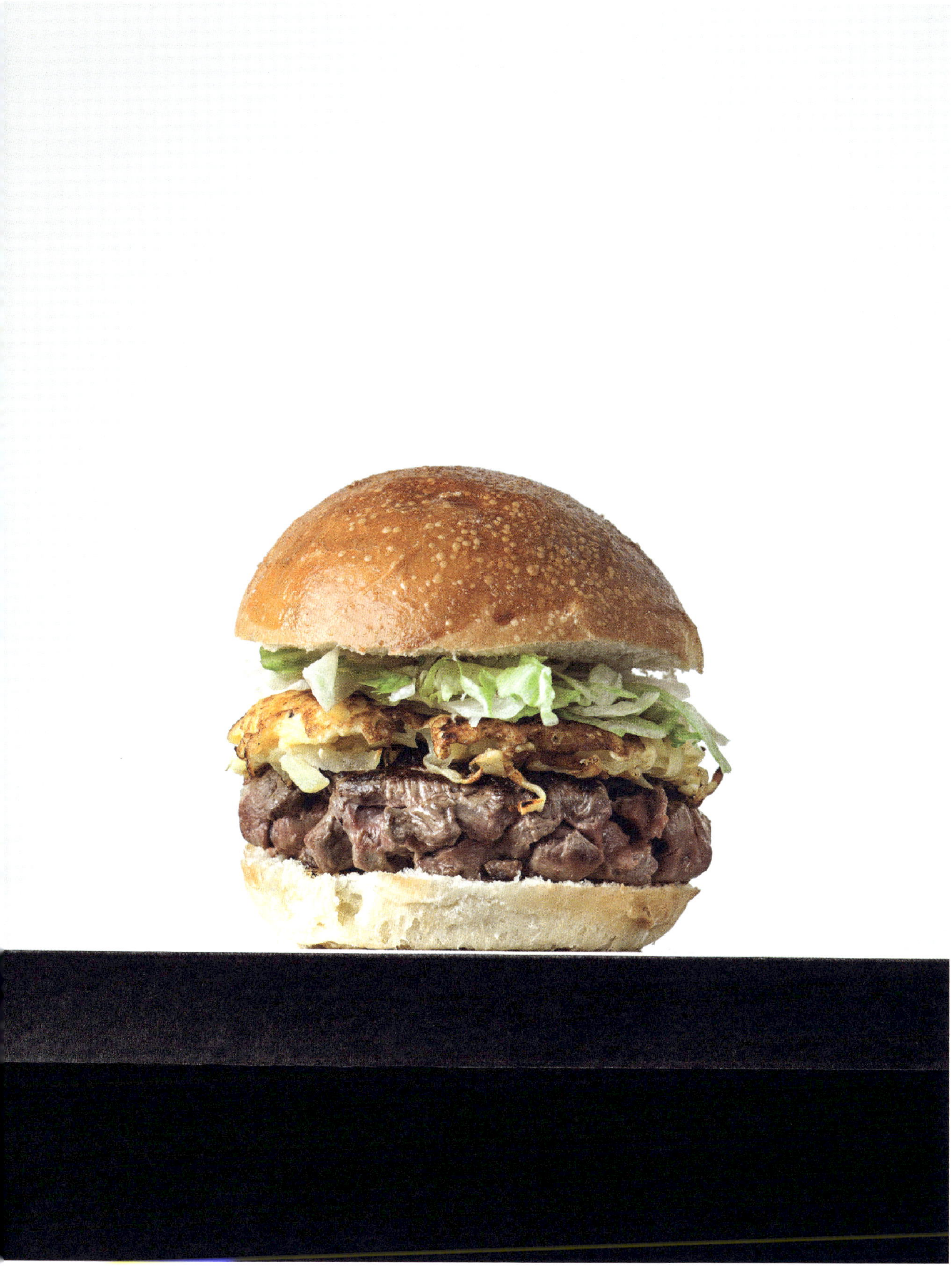

RECIPE NO. 23

FISH
CLASSIC WITH AIOLI

Level of difficulty: ●●●
Preparation time: 30 mins
Number of hamburgers: 4

Type of fish

COD

BUNS
homemade or bought buns	4

PATTIES
cod, barramundi or other firm, white-fleshed fish	500 g (1 lb 2 oz)
lemon (juice)	1
salt	1 pinch
olive oil	1 drizzle
plain (all-purpose) flour	100 g (3½ oz/⅔ cup)
eggs, beaten	2
dry breadcrumbs	100 g (3½ oz)
butter	1 knob
oil	a splash

AIOLI SAUCE
garlic, crushed	3 cloves
mustard	1 tablespoon
egg yolk	1
salt	1 pinch
pepper	1 pinch
olive oil	1 tablespoon

TOPPINGS
rocket (arugula)	a large handful

BUNS
Make the buns as described on page 14 or use ready-made buns.

PATTIES
Cut the cod into small pieces with a knife. Form into 4 patties, using a ring mould, making sure they stick together well. The patties should be firm so they don't fall apart. Season them with the lemon juice, salt and olive oil. Put the flour, beaten eggs and breadcrumbs in three separate bowls. Crumb the patties by dipping them first in the flour, then in the egg, then in the breadcrumbs. Set them aside in the refrigerator for the time it takes to prepare the rest.

AIOLI SAUCE
Put the garlic, mustard, egg yolk, salt and pepper in a bowl. Beat with an electric beater, gradually pouring in the olive oil until you have a light, but thick, consistency.

COOKING THE PATTIES
Preheat the oven to 200°C (400°F/Gas 6). Add the butter and oil to a hot frying pan over medium heat and cook the patties for about 3–4 minutes per side. Transfer the patties to a lightly greased baking tray and cook in the oven for a further 5 minutes.

ASSEMBLY
Cut the buns in half horizontally and toast them for 2 minutes under the grill (broiler). Put the cod patties on the cut side of the bun heels, then divide the aïoli and rocket between them. Finish with the crowns.

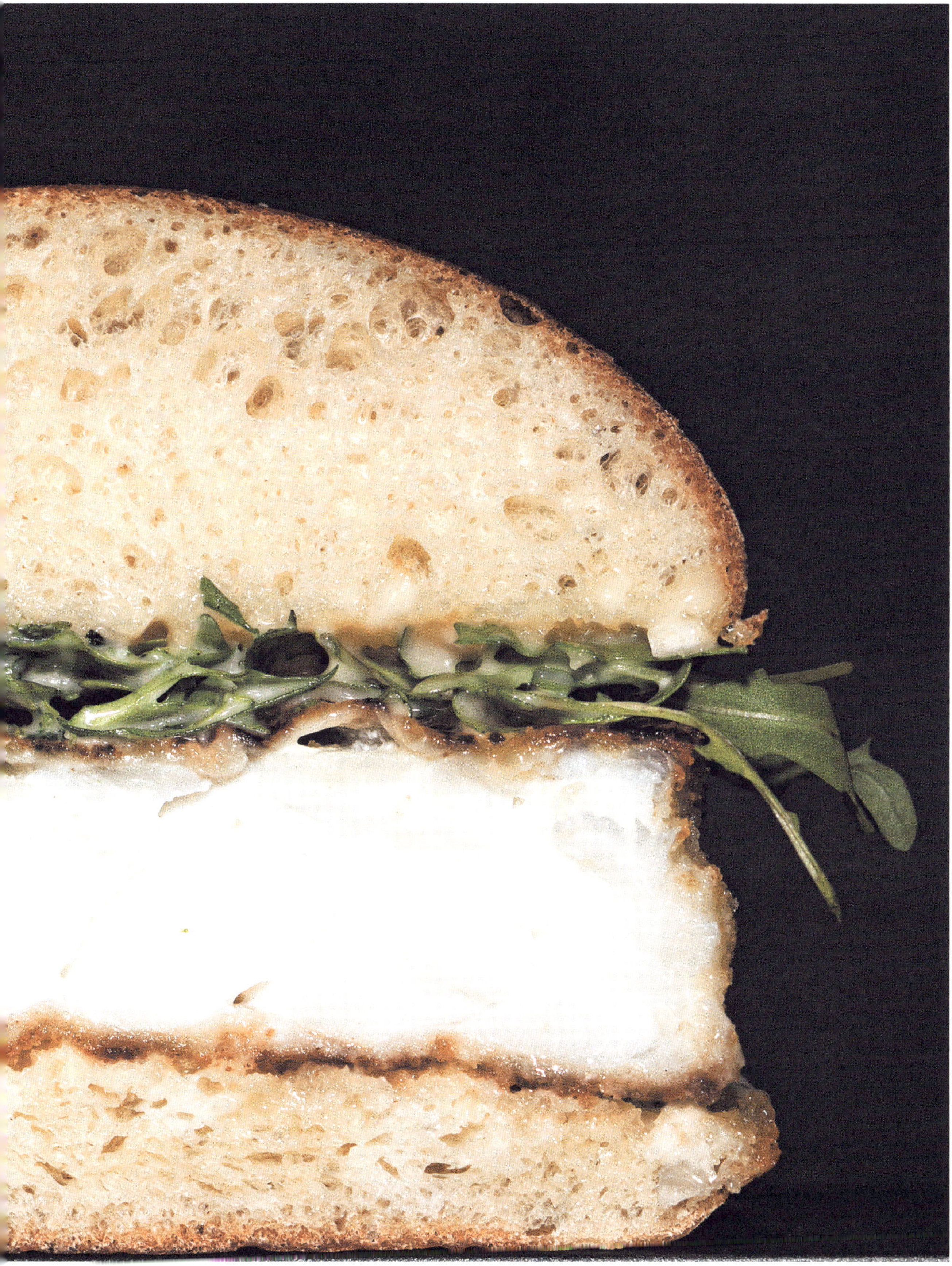

RECIPE NO. 24

SALMON

SALMON, DILL, LEMON

Level of difficulty: ●●
Preparation time: 20 mins + 15 mins refrigeration time
Number of hamburgers: 4

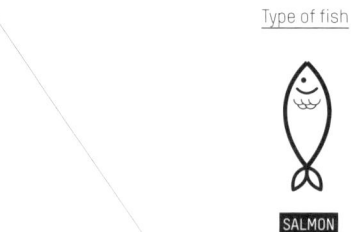

Type of fish

SALMON

BUNS
homemade or bought buns	4

PATTIES
fresh salmon fillet, bones removed	600 g (1 lb 5 oz)
butter	1 knob

SAUCE
dill, chopped	½ bunch
crème fraîche	200 g (7 oz)
lemon (juice)	1
salt	1 pinch
pepper	1 pinch

TOPPINGS
rocket (arugula)	a large handful

BUNS
Make the buns as described on page 14 or use ready-made buns.

PATTIES
Lay the salmon fillet out flat. Hold the knife blade horizontally and carve the salmon into slices approximately 3 mm ($1/8$ inch) thick. Cut across these slices so you have pieces about the size of a credit card. Lay the slices on top of each other to form a patty the same diameter as the bread—the easiest way is to stack them inside a cookie cutter. Press firmly with the palm of your hand, then refrigerate for at least 15 minutes. Preheat the oven to 180°C (350°F/Gas 4).

SAUCE
In a bowl, combine the dill, crème fraîche and lemon juice. Season with the salt and pepper.

COOKING THE PATTIES
Add the butter to a hot frying pan heated over high heat and brown the patties for about 1 minute on each side. Put the patties on a lightly greased baking tray and finish cooking in the oven for about 4 minutes.

ASSEMBLY
Cut the buns in half horizontally and toast them for 2 minutes under the grill (broiler). Spread the cut side of the bun heels with the dill sauce, add the patties and a few rocket leaves. Finish with the crowns.

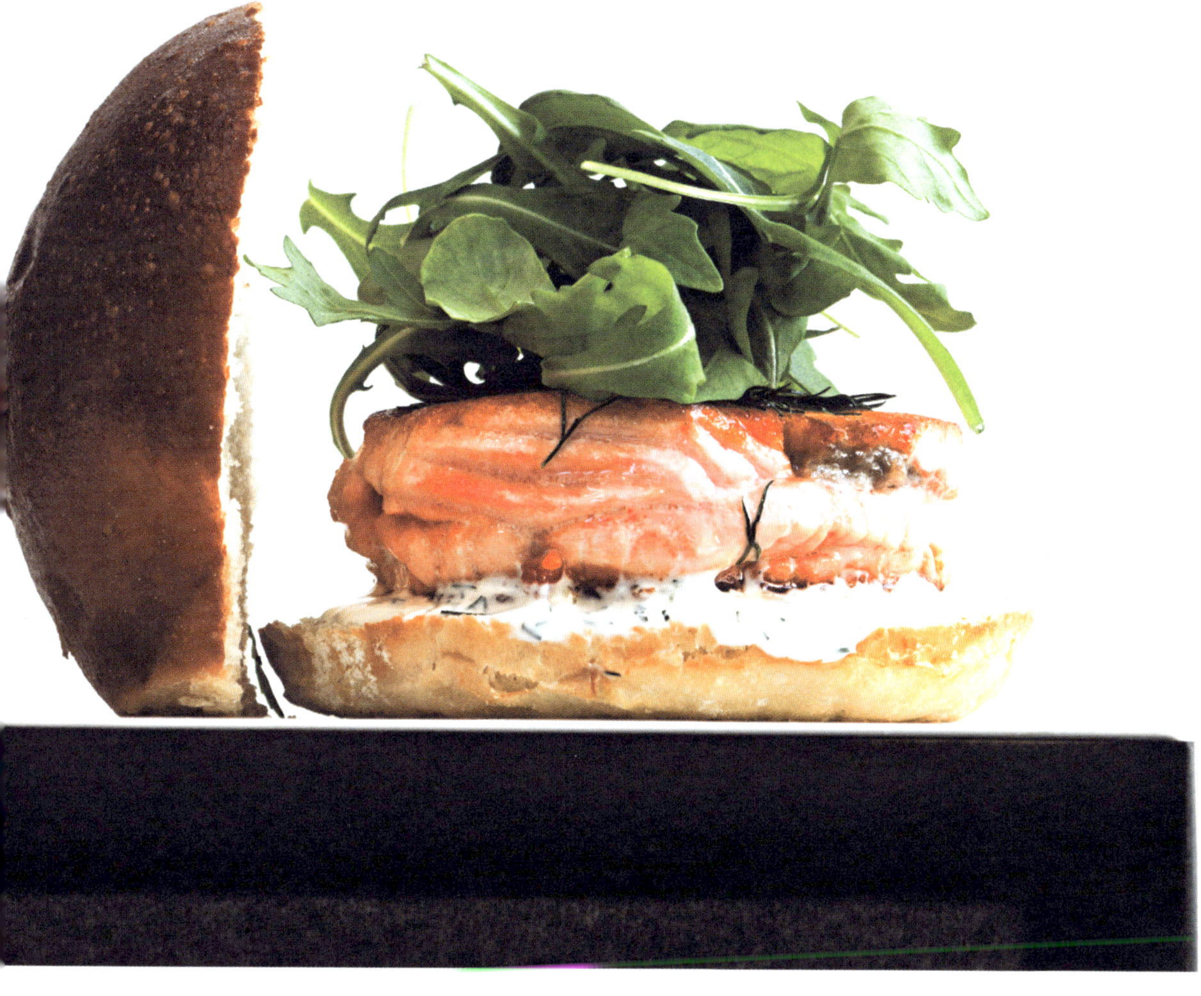

RECIPE NO. 25

SPICY
SPICY TUNA

Level of difficulty:
Preparation time: 50 mins
Number of hamburgers: 4

Type of fish

TUNA

BUNS
homemade or bought buns 4

PATTIES
tuna steaks
    4 small, about 140 g (5 oz) each
olive oil .... 1 drizzle

RELISH 1
red capsicums (peppers), seeded, membranes removed and cut into chunks 2
tomato, diced 1
water .... 3 tablespoons
small cayenne chilli pepper 1

RELISH 2
olive oil .... 1 tablespoon
onions, thinly sliced 2
caster sugar .... 50 g (1¾ oz)

TOPPINGS
flat-leaf (Italian) parsley leaves .... ½ cup

BUNS
Make the buns as described on page 14 or use ready-made buns.

PATTIES
Cut the tuna into rounds with a ring cutter.

RELISH 1
Put the capsicum and diced tomato in a saucepan over medium heat, add the water and the cayenne pepper whole so you can remove it later. Stew together for about 30 minutes, stirring occasionally. Season with sea salt and freshly ground black pepper.

RELISH 2
Heat the olive oil in a saucepan and cook the onion for 3 minutes over medium heat, covered. Remove the lid and add the sugar when the onion starts to brown. Stop cooking when well caramelised: allow about 8 minutes in all.

COOKING THE PATTIES
Pour the olive oil into a hot frying pan and sear the tuna steaks for about 1 minute on each side—tuna is usually seared briefly on each side.

ASSEMBLY
Cut the buns in half horizontally and toast them for 2 minutes under the grill (broiler). Spread half of the tomato-capsicum relish over the cut side of the bun heels. Add the caramelised onion, the tuna patties, the parsley and the remaining relish. Finish with the crowns.

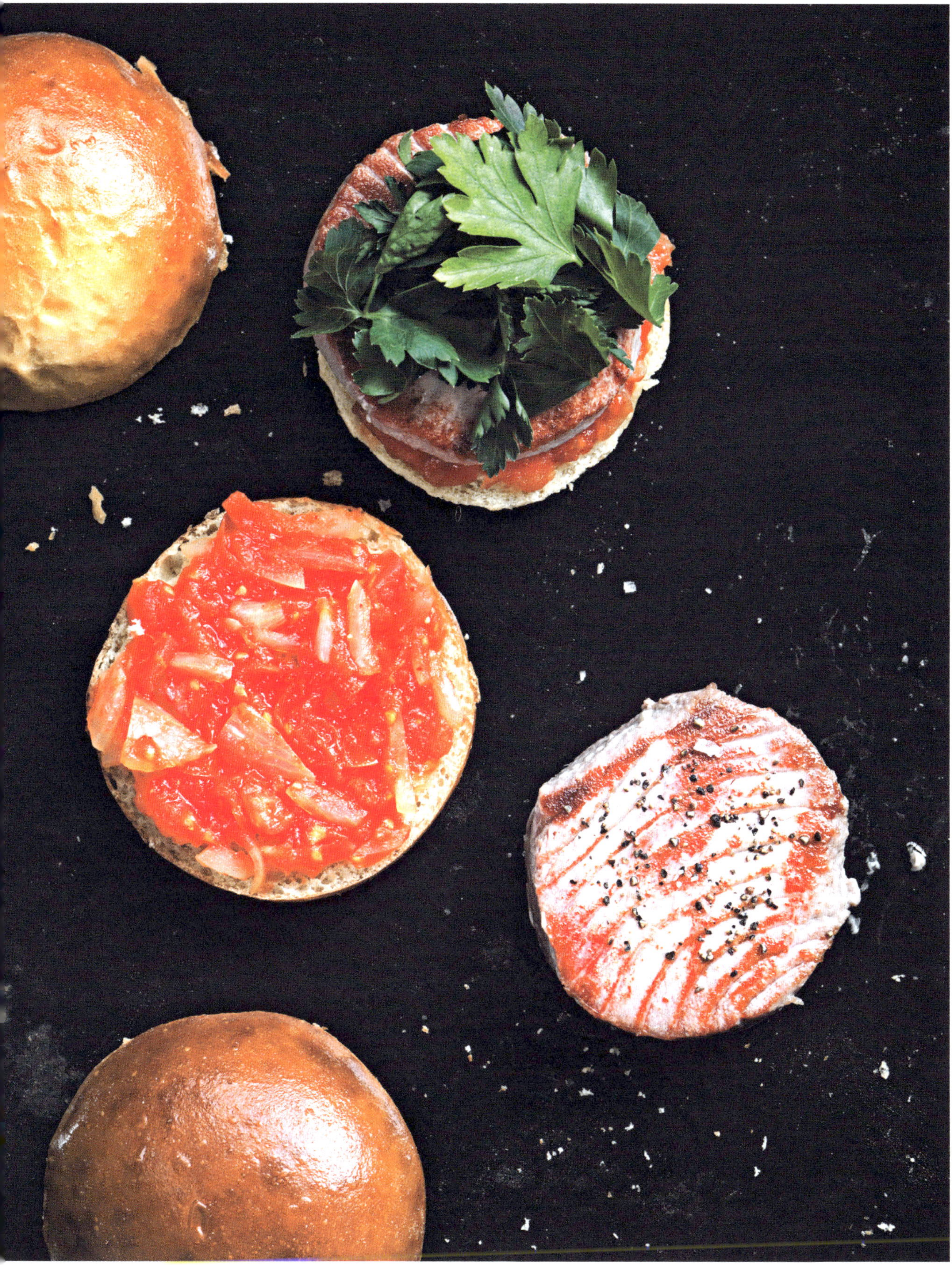

RECIPE NO. 26

THAI
THAI PRAWN

Level of difficulty: ●●●
Preparation time: 30 mins
Number of hamburgers: 4

Type of fish: PRAWN

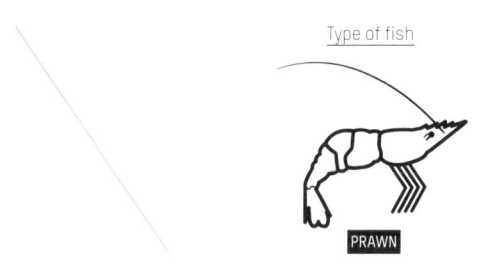

BUNS
homemade or bought buns 4

PATTIES
prawns (shrimp), peeled, cooked and thinly sliced 16

SAUCE
crème fraîche ..... 200 g (7 oz)
wasabi ..... 2 teaspoons
soy sauce ..... 2 teaspoons

TOPPINGS
rocket (arugula) ..... a large handful

BUNS
Make the buns as described on page 14 or use ready-made buns.

PATTIES
Take 4 round cookie cutters, roughly the size of the buns, and arrange the slices of prawn on top of each other to form 4 nicely rounded patties. Preheat the oven to 180°C (350°F/Gas 4).

SAUCE
Put the crème fraîche in a bowl. Add the wasabi and soy sauce. Whisk together and set aside in the refrigerator until the burgers are ready to be assembled.

COOKING THE PATTIES
Without removing the cookie cutters, put the patties on a lightly greased baking tray and cook in the oven for 5 minutes.

ASSEMBLY
Cut the buns in half horizontally and toast them for 2 minutes under the grill (broiler). Spread the cut side of the bun heels with half of the sauce. Add the patties, then the rest of the sauce and the rocket leaves. Finish with the crowns.

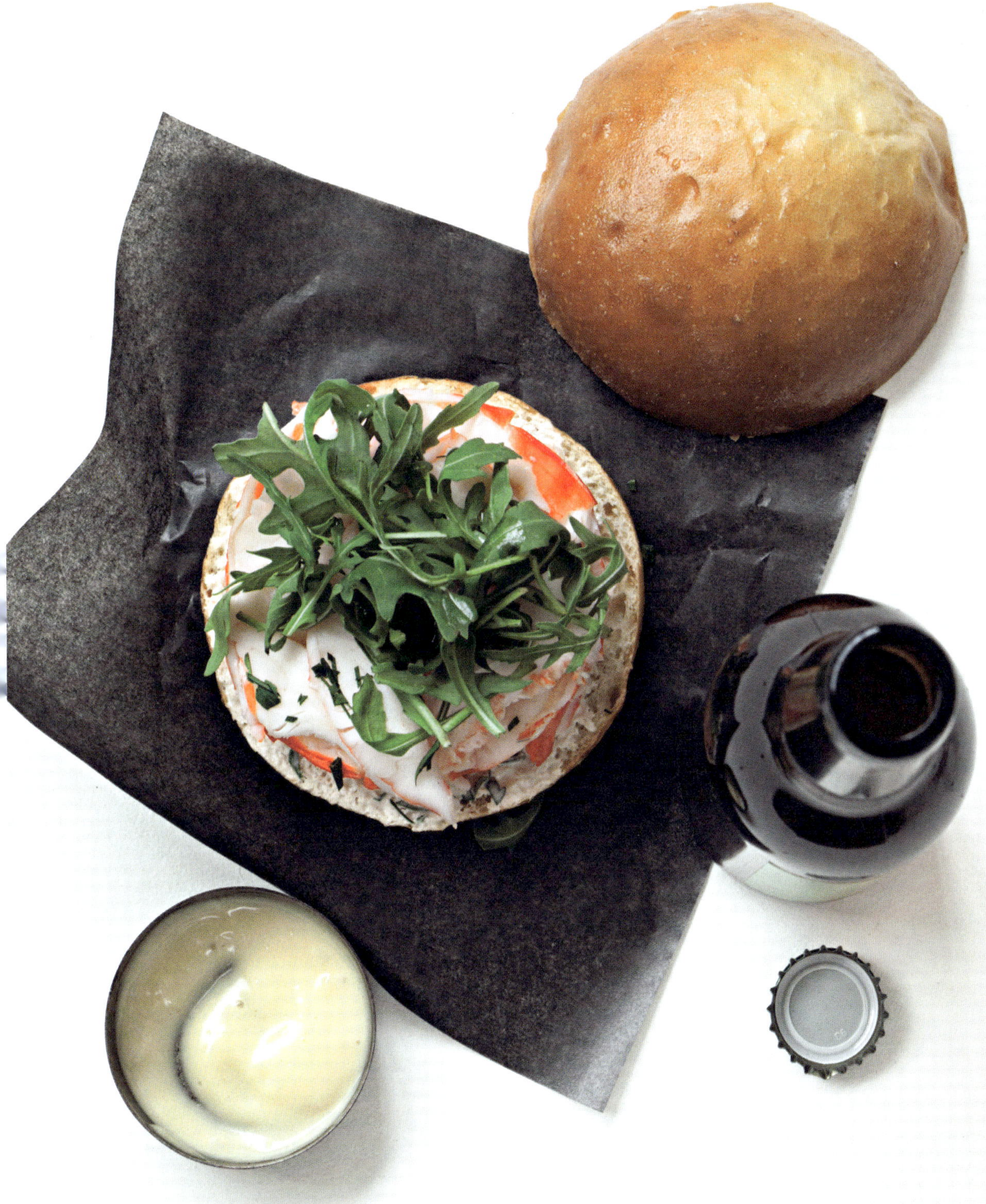

RECIPE NO. 27

COD

CRUMBED COD, ESCABÈCHE SAUCE

Level of difficulty:
Preparation time: 30 mins + 10 mins refrigeration time
Number of hamburgers: 4

Type of fish

COD

BUNS

| homemade or bought buns | 4 |

PATTIES

cod fillets	4 x 125 g (4½ oz)
plain (all-purpose) flour	100 g (3½ oz/⅔ cup)
eggs, beaten	2
dry breadcrumbs	100 g (3½ oz)
olive oil	1 drizzle

SAUCE

garlic, coarsely chopped	7 or 8 cloves
parsley, chopped	1 sprig
olive oil	2 tablespoons
red peppercorns, in brine	1 teaspoon
dried bay leaves	2 or 3
vinegar	1 port glass
salt	1 pinch
pepper	1 pinch
tomato paste (concentrated purée)	25 g (1 oz)

TOPPINGS

| baby spinach | 45 g (1¾ oz/1 cup) |

BUNS

Make the buns as described on page 14 or use ready-made buns.

PATTIES

Cut the cod fillets into pieces the size of the bun and crumb them by dipping each piece first into the flour, then in the beaten egg, then in the breadcrumbs. Once crumbed, set aside in the refrigerator for at least 10 minutes.

SAUCE

In a frying pan over medium heat, sweat the garlic with the parsley in the olive oil. Add the remaining ingredients and simmer for 8–10 minutes.

COOKING THE PATTIES

Heat the olive oil in a frying pan and brown each piece of cod by cooking in the pan for 2–3 minutes on each side, or until cooked through.

ASSEMBLY

Cut the buns in half horizontally and toast them for 2 minutes under the grill (broiler). Spread the cut side of the bun heels with half of the sauce, put the crumbed cod on top and spread with the remaining sauce, then add the spinach. Top with the crowns.

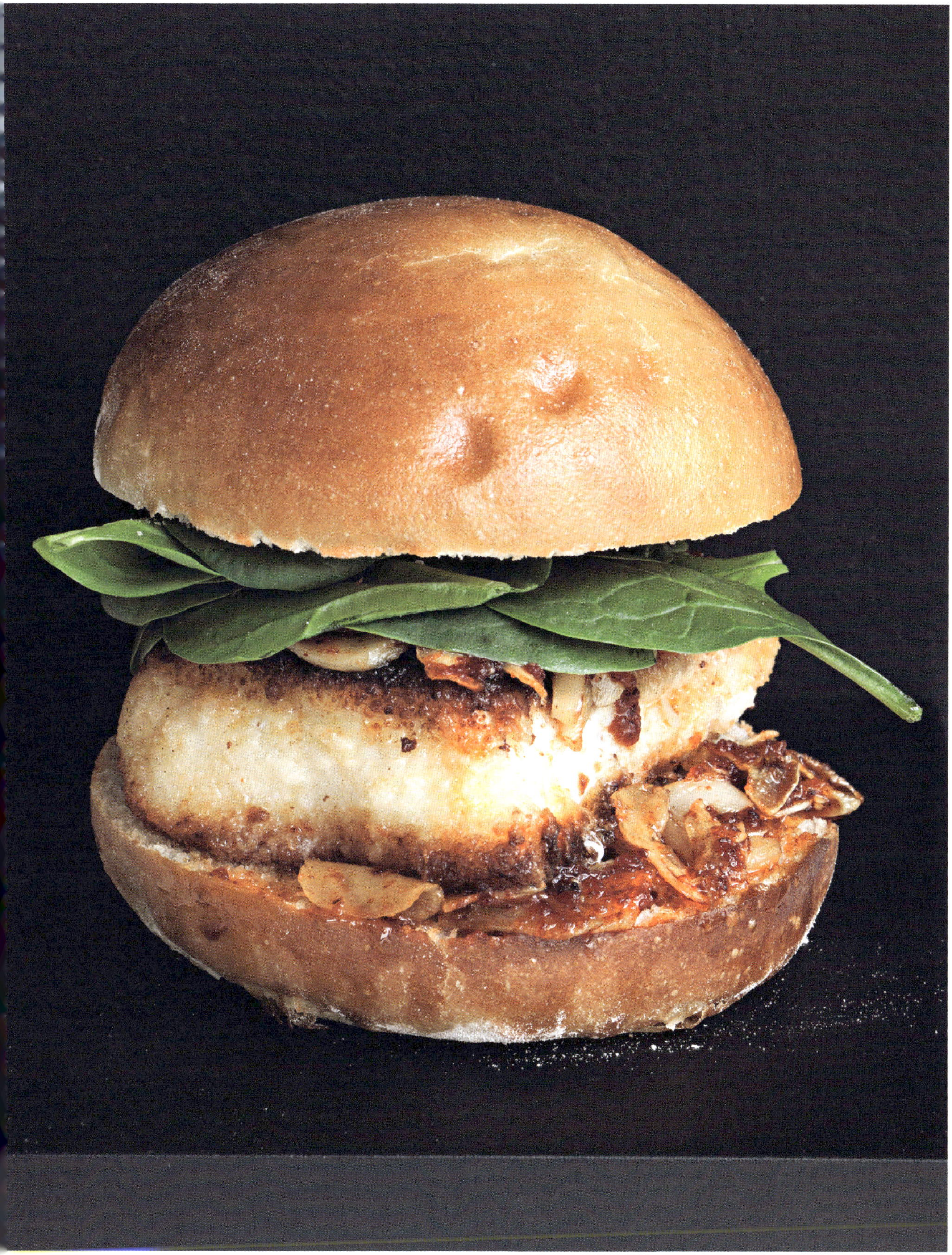

RECIPE NO. 28

ACE
THE CLASSIC WITH PIG

Level of difficulty:
Preparation time: 30 mins
Number of hamburgers: 4

Type of meat

PIG

BUNS
homemade or bought buns	4

PATTIES
pork, minced (ground)	500 g (1 lb 2 oz)
sea salt	a few pinches

TOPPINGS
pineapple	½ large
caster sugar	50 g (1¾ oz)
fresh mint	40 g (1½ oz)

BUNS
Make the buns as described on page 14 or use ready-made buns.

PATTIES
Form 4 patties from the minced pork and season them with the sea salt.

TOPPINGS
Peel and core the pineapple, then cut it into 1.5 cm (⅝ inch) even slices. Put the slices in a frying pan over low heat and gradually add the sugar. Cook for about 10 minutes until the pineapple slices are lightly browned. Chop half the mint, reserving the other half for the assembly stage. Sprinkle the pineapple with the chopped mint.

COOKING THE PATTIES
Cook the patties in a hot frying pan over high heat, 5 minutes per side.

ASSEMBLY
Cut the buns in half horizontally and toast them for 2 minutes under the grill (broiler). Divide half of the pineapple slices between the cut side of the bun heels, add the patties, then the rest of the pineapple and the mint leaves. Top with the crowns.

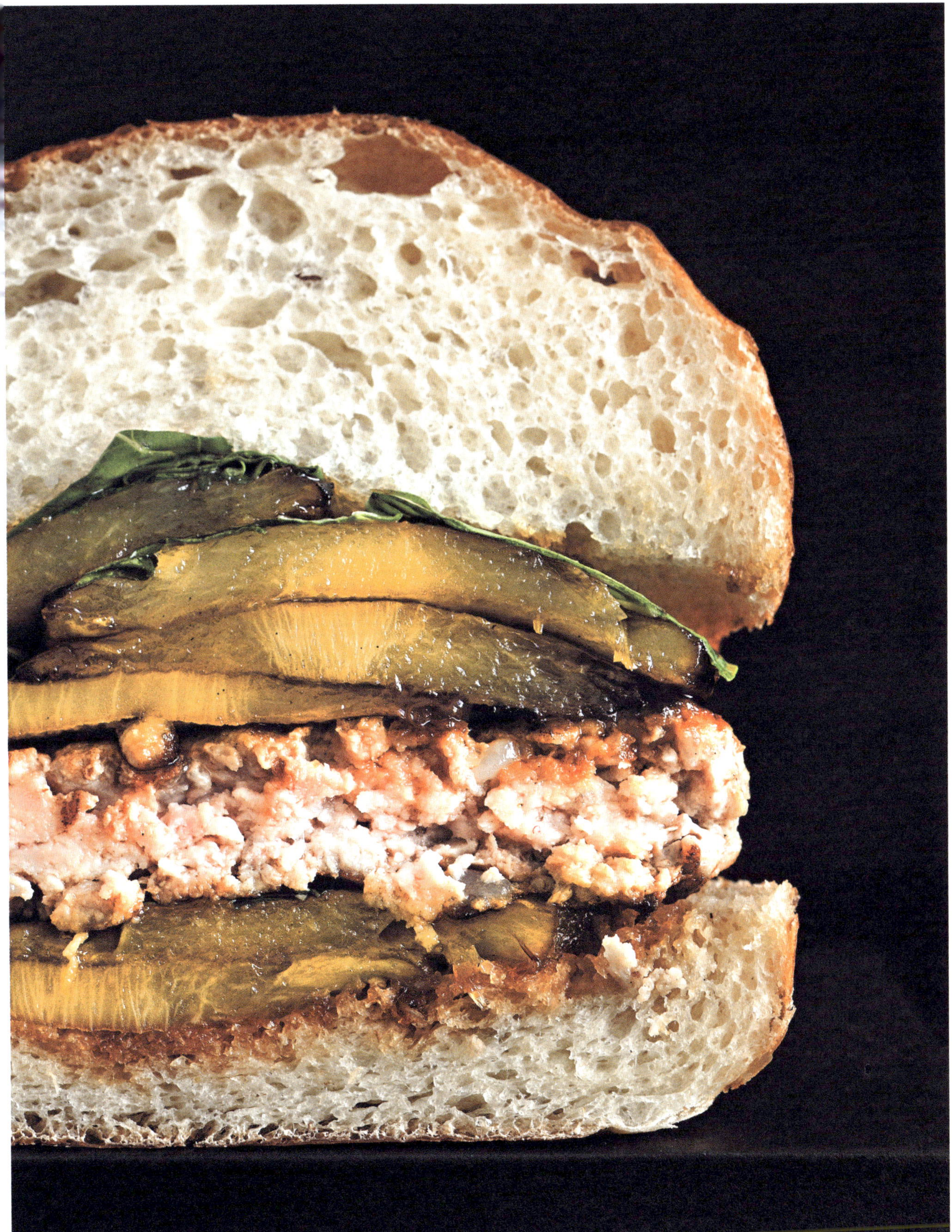

RECIPE NO. 29

RADISH
PIG, BLACK RADISH

Level of difficulty: ●●
Preparation time: 35 mins
Number of hamburgers: 4

Type of meat

PIG

BUNS
homemade or bought buns — 4

PATTIES
pork, minced (ground) — 500 g (1 lb 2 oz)
sea salt — a few pinches

RELISH
carrots, peeled and cut into thin sticks — 2
black radish or daikon, peeled and cut into thin sticks — ¾
olive oil — 100 ml (3½ fl oz)

RADISH CHIPS
black radish or daikon, cut into thin rounds — 1
olive oil — 1 drizzle

TOPPINGS
rocket (arugula) — a large handful

BUNS
Make the buns as described on page 14 or use ready-made buns.

PATTIES
Form 4 patties from the minced pork and season them with the sea salt.

RELISH
Stew the carrot and radish in a saucepan with the olive oil over low heat for 10 minutes, or until softened. Drain and season.

BLACK RADISH CHIPS
In a frying pan, sauté the radish rounds, in batches, with the olive oil for 10–15 minutes over medium heat, turning often to make them into crisps. Drain on paper towels.

COOKING THE PATTIES
Cook the patties in a hot frying pan over high heat, 5 minutes per side.

ASSEMBLY
Cut the buns in half horizontally and toast them for 2 minutes under the grill (broiler). Top the cut side of the bun heels with half of the relish, add the patties, then the remaining relish, the radish chips and the rocket. Top with the crowns.

UNE RECETTE
DE STEAK-HACHE
YVES
MARIE LE
SELON
DE PARIS
L'EXPRESS
D'APRÈS

2

MIX / COMBINATIONS OF MEATS AND SPICES

Combinations of Meat and Spices

RECIPE NO. 30

BLUE
BLUE CHEESE, BASIL

Level of difficulty:
Preparation time: 30 mins
Number of hamburgers: 4

Type of meat

BEEF

BUNS
homemade or bought buns 4

PATTIES
Bleu d'Auvergne, or other strong blue cheese
.... 60 g (2¼ oz)
beef, minced (ground)   500 g (1 lb 2 oz)
sea salt .... a few pinches

SAUCE
basil .... 50 g (1¾ oz)
thin (pouring) cream
.... 80 ml (2½ fl oz/⅓ cup)
crème fraîche .... 85 g (3 oz/⅓ cup)
garlic, chopped .... 1 clove
Bleu d'Auvergne, sliced ...... 200 g (7 oz)

BUNS
Make the buns as described on page 14 or use ready-made buns.

PATTIES
Cut the well-chilled Bleu d'Auvergne into small cubes. Incorporate them into the minced beef and form 4 patties. Season them with the sea salt.

SAUCE
Chop most of the basil; set aside about a dozen leaves for the assembly stage. Put the two creams in a saucepan and boil them with the garlic and chopped basil. Simmer for about 5 minutes or until the sauce begins to thicken. Off the heat, add the Bleu d'Auvergne and melt it in, stirring if necessary. Cool, then set aside in the refrigerator until needed.

COOKING THE PATTIES
Cook the patties in a hot frying pan over high heat, 3 minutes per side for rare patties.

ASSEMBLY
Cut the buns in half horizontally and toast them for 2 minutes under the grill (broiler). On the cut side of the bun heels put the patties, blue cheese and basil sauce and the reserved basil leaves. Top with the bun crowns.

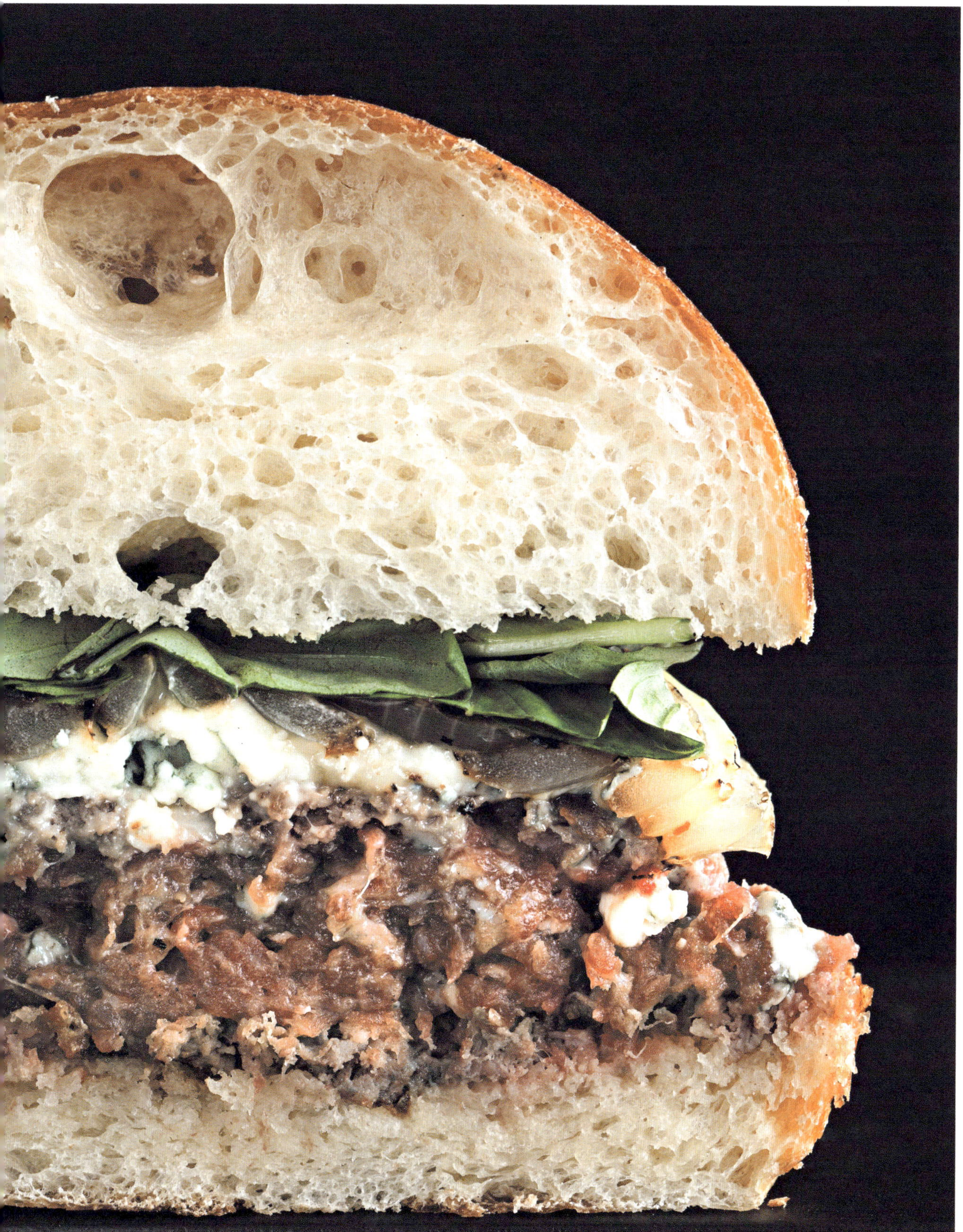

RECIPE NO. 31

SCOTCH
BEEF WITH WHISKY

Level of difficulty:
Preparation time: 35 mins + 10 mins refrigeration time
Number of hamburgers: 4

Type of meat

BEEF

BUNS
homemade or bought buns	4

PATTIES
beef, minced (ground)	500 g (1 lb 2 oz)
bourbon	2 teaspoons
sea salt	a few pinches

SAUCE
water	60 ml (2 fl oz/¼ cup)
vintage cheddar cheese	100 g (3½ oz)
green capsicum (pepper), seeded and membrane removed	1

TOPPINGS
olive oil	1–2 tablespoons
green capsicum (pepper), seeded and membrane removed, cut into strips	1
onion, thinly sliced	1
bourbon	2 tablespoons
rocket (arugula)	a large handful

BUNS
Make the buns as described on page 14 or use ready-made buns.

PATTIES
Incorporate the bourbon into the minced beef. Make 4 patties. Set aside in the refrigerator for 10 minutes.

SAUCE
Heat the water in a saucepan over low heat. Cut the cheddar into small cubes and add gradually to the water, stirring to melt the cheese. Dice the capsicum and add to the mixture.

TOPPINGS
Heat the olive oil in a deep frying pan over high heat. Brown the capsicum and onion together. After 10 minutes of cooking, flambé by adding the bourbon.

COOKING THE PATTIES
Season the patties with the sea salt and cook in a hot frying pan. Cook for 3 minutes each side for rare patties.

ASSEMBLY
Cut the buns in half horizontally and toast them for 2 minutes under the grill (broiler). On the cut side of the bun heels put the flambéd onion and capsicum, the patties, the melted cheddar sauce and a few rocket leaves. Top with the crowns.

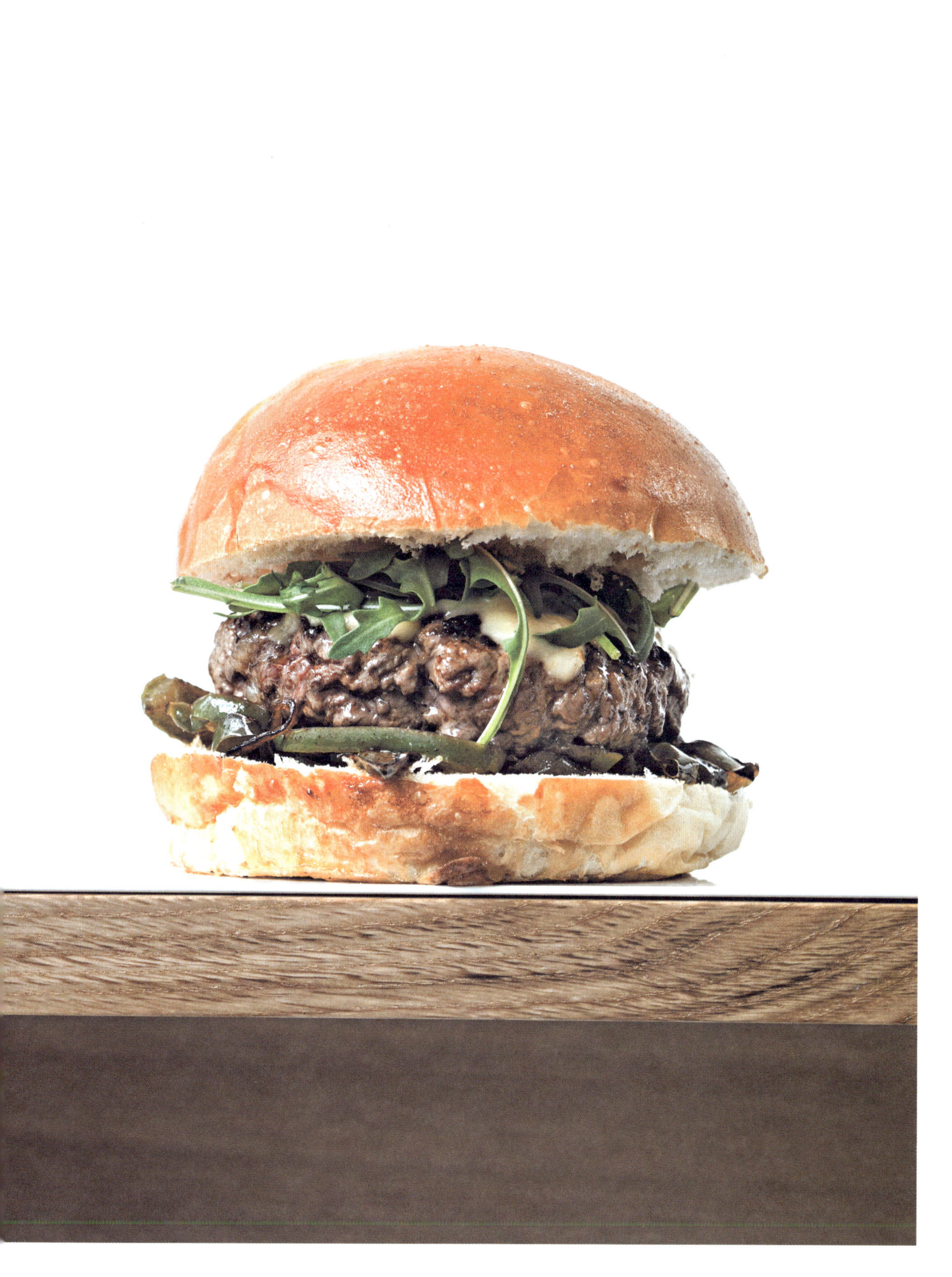

RECIPE NO. 32

RING

SMOKY BEEF, ONION RINGS

Level of difficulty:
Preparation time: 40 mins
Number of hamburgers: 4

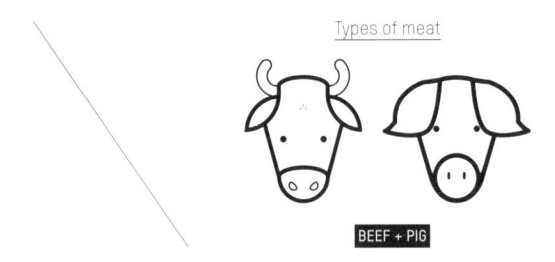

Types of meat

BEEF + PIG

BUNS
homemade or bought buns — 4

PATTIES
beef, minced (ground) — 500 g (1 lb 2 oz)
smoked pork belly, diced — 100 g (3½ oz)

ONION RINGS
large onion, sliced into rings — ½
plain (all-purpose) flour — 100 g (3½ oz/⅔ cup)
egg, separated — 1
milk — 100 ml (3½ fl oz)
olive oil — 200 ml (7 fl oz)
salt — 1 pinch
vegetable oil — for deep-frying

TOPPINGS
tomatoes, sliced — 2
olive oil — a splash
barbecue sauce (see page 26) — 120 ml (4 fl oz)
iceberg lettuce, shredded — a few leaves

BUNS
Make the buns as described on page 14 or use ready-made buns.

PATTIES
To give the beef a smoky flavour, add the pork belly. Cut out 4 rounds from it with a cookie cutter—you will use these when cooking the patties. Make 4 patties from the minced beef.

ONION RINGS
Separate the onion slices. Mix the flour, egg yolk, milk, olive oil and salt to a smooth paste. Gently fold in the egg white, whipped to soft peaks. Dip the onion rings in the batter so they are well coated then fry them in a deep-fryer or a frying pan with oil heated to 180°C (350°F) (or until a cube of bread dropped into the oil browns in 15 seconds) for 3 minutes. Drain the onion rings on paper towels to remove excess oil.

TOPPINGS
Season the tomatoes, then cook them in a frying pan with a little olive oil over high heat, 2 minutes each side.

COOKING THE PATTIES
Put the pork belly rounds on the patties, cover with a stainless steel bowl and cook over a medium heat for 4 minutes on each side.

ASSEMBLY
Cut the buns in half horizontally and toast them for 2 minutes under the grill (broiler). Spread the cut side of the bun heels with the barbecue sauce, add the tomato slices, the patties, the onion rings and the iceberg lettuce. Top with the crowns.

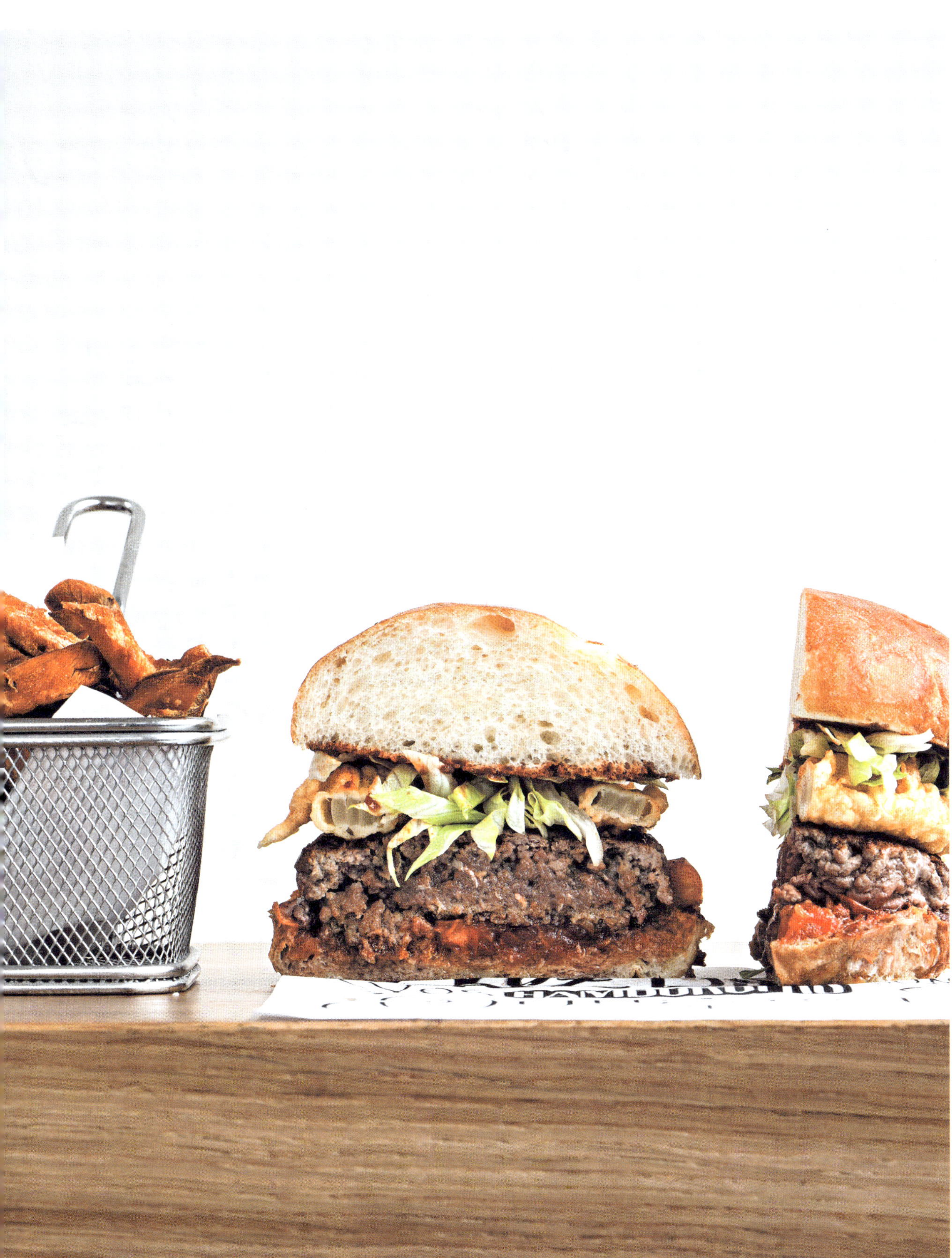

RECIPE NO. 33

BEER
BEEF WITH BEER

Level of difficulty:
Preparation time: 40 mins + 10 mins refrigeration time
Number of hamburgers: 4

Type of meat

BEEF

BUNS

| homemade or bought buns | 4 |

SAUCE

onion, finely diced	½
garlic, chopped	3 cloves
worcestershire sauce	1 tablespoon
beer	3 tablespoons

PATTIES

beef, minced (ground)	500 g (1 lb 2 oz)
sheep's milk cheese, cut into small cubes	50 g (1¾ oz)
sea salt	a few pinches

RELISH

onion, finely diced	½
olive oil	1 drizzle
sugar	1 tablespoon

TOPPINGS

| iceberg lettuce, finely shredded | ¼ |

BUNS

Make the buns as described on page 14 or use ready-made buns.

SAUCE

In a bowl, combine the onion, garlic, worcestershire sauce and beer, then let stand for at least 10 minutes.

PATTIES

Combine half the sauce with the minced beef. Form 4 patties and set them aside in the refrigerator for at least 10 minutes.

RELISH

Caramelise the onion in a frying pan over medium heat for 10 minutes with the olive oil. Add the sugar when the onion starts to brown.

COOKING THE PATTIES

Season the patties with the sea salt. In a hot frying pan, cook the patties over high heat. After 3 minutes of cooking, turn them over, distribute the cubes of cheese on top and cover with a stainless steel bowl. When the cheese starts to melt, add a little onion relish.

ASSEMBLY

Cut the buns in half horizontally and toast them for 2 minutes under the grill (broiler). Spread the cut side of the bun heels with the beer sauce, add the rest of the relish, the patties with the cheese, the remaining beer sauce and the shredded iceberg lettuce. Finish with the bun crowns.

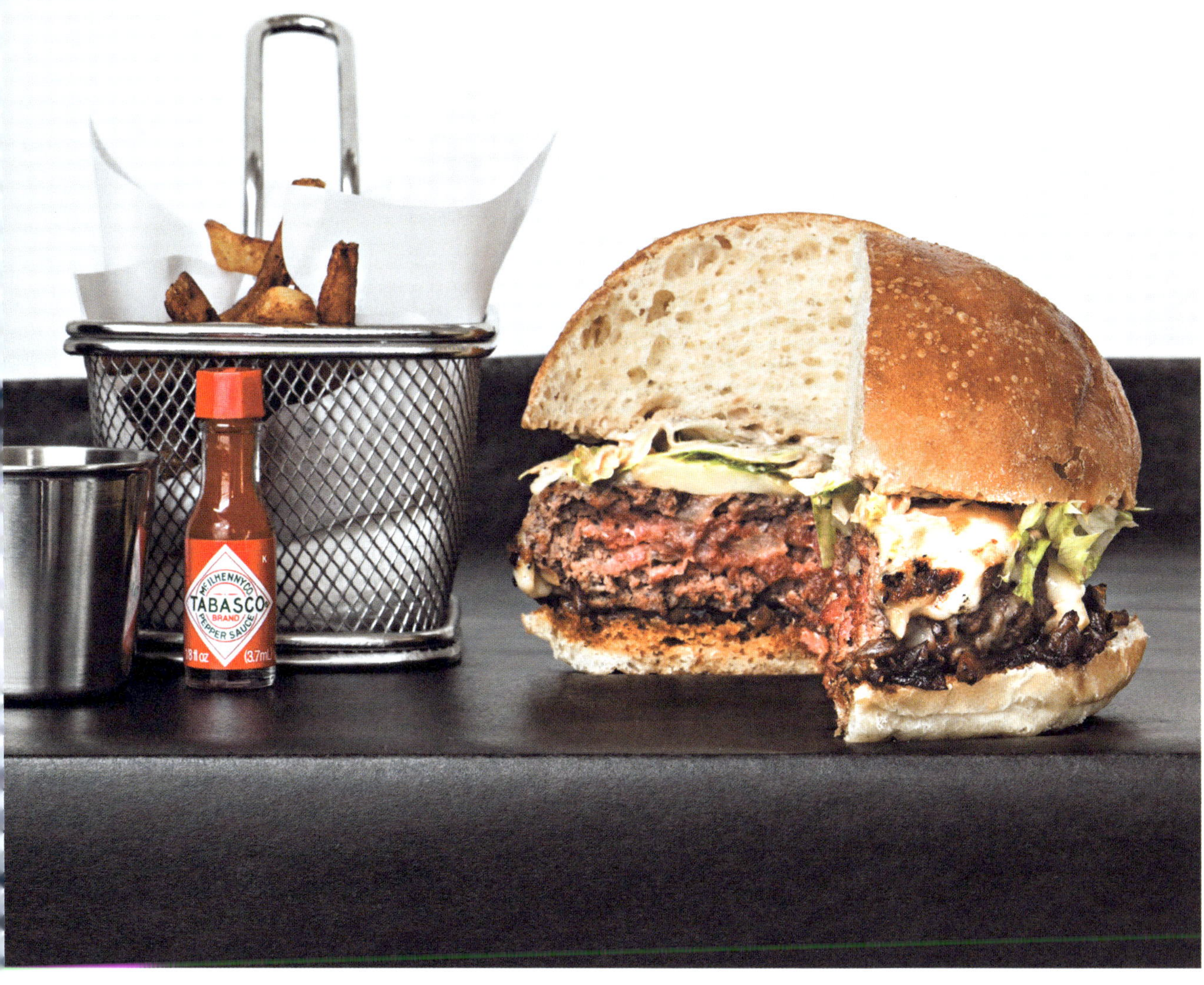
TABASCO
BRAND
PEPPER SAUCE

RECIPE NO. 34

DIABLO
SPICY BEEF, BACON

Level of difficulty:
Preparation time: 35 mins + 2 hours refrigeration time
Number of hamburgers: 4

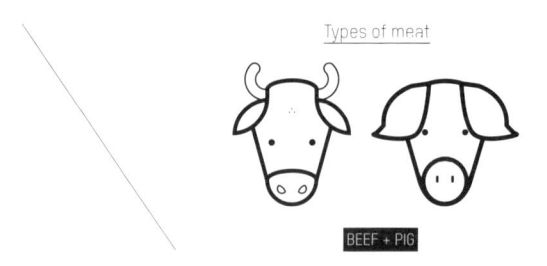

Types of meat

BEEF + PIG

BUNS
homemade or bought buns	4

PATTIES
beef, minced (ground)	500 g (1 lb 2 oz)
onion, finely chopped	1
parsley, chopped	a few leaves
worcestershire sauce	2 teaspoons
Mexican chilli, chopped	1 tablespoon
salt	1 pinch
pepper	1 pinch
cayenne pepper	½ teaspoon
cheddar cheese, grated	45 g (1¾ oz/½ cup)

SPICY SAUCE
mayonnaise	2 teaspoons
crème fraîche	2 teaspoons
fresh coriander (cilantro) leaves	2 sprigs
lemon juice	1 tablespoon
onion, finely chopped	4
Mexican chilli, chopped	1 tablespoon
cayenne pepper	½ teaspoon
salt	1 pinch
pepper	1 pinch

TOPPINGS
bacon	200 g (7 oz)
rocket (arugula)	a few leaves

BUNS
Make the buns as described on page 14 or use ready-made buns.

PATTIES
Combine all of the ingredients except the cheese in a large bowl. Form 4 patties and put them in the refrigerator for at least 2 hours.

SPICY SAUCE
Blend all the ingredients together in a food processor. Season with extra salt and pepper if needed.

TOPPINGS
Heat a frying pan and cook the bacon for about 10 minutes until crispy.

COOKING THE PATTIES
Season the patties with sea salt and cook them for 3 minutes on each side. Put the cheddar cheese on top of the patties at the end of the cooking time and cover with a stainless steel bowl until the cheddar melts.

ASSEMBLY
Cut the buns in half horizontally and toast them for 2 minutes under the grill (broiler). Spread the cut side of the heels and crowns with half of the spicy sauce. On the bun heels put the patties with cheese, the bacon, rocket and the remaining spicy sauce. Top with the crowns.

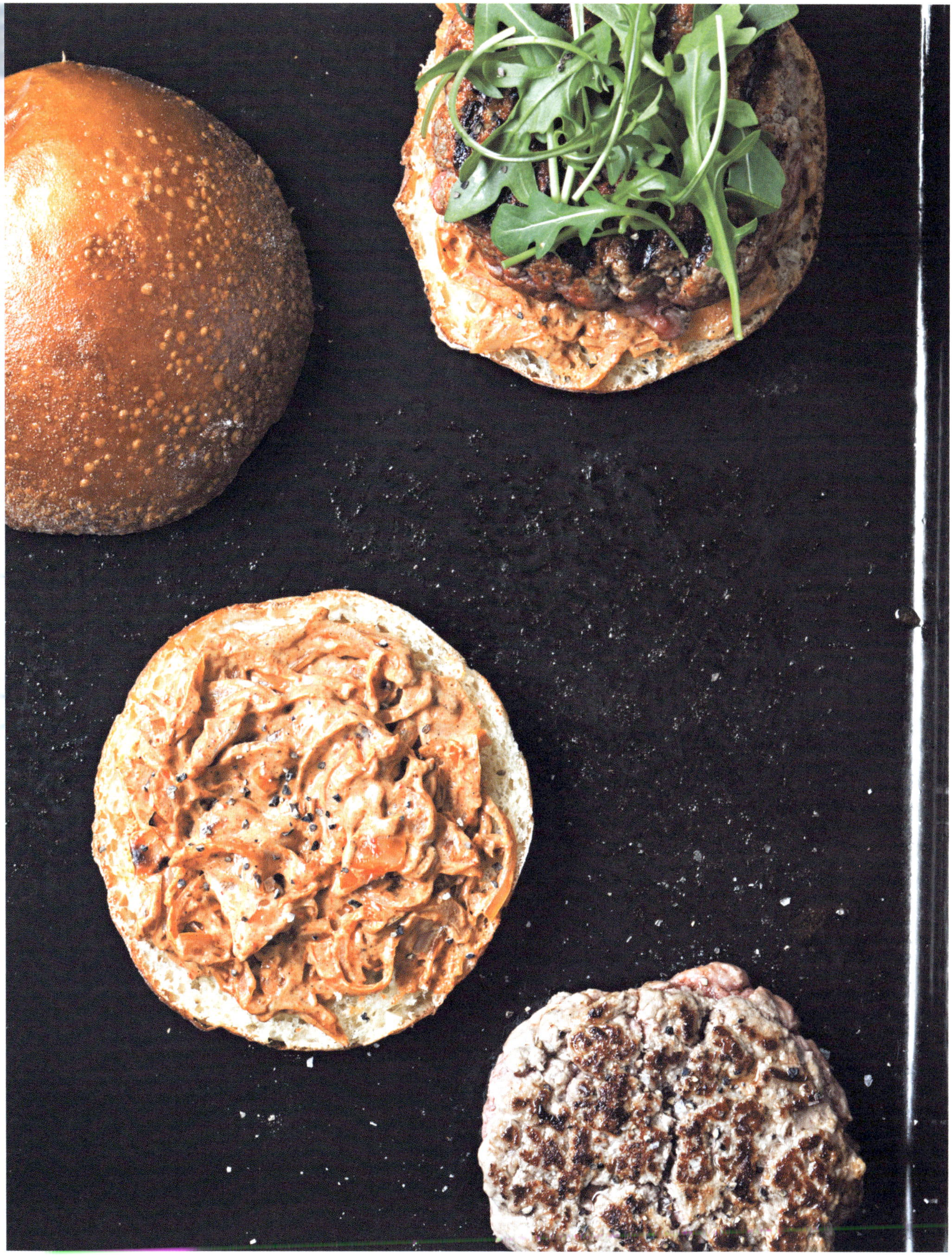

RECIPE NO. 35

PESTO
BEEF WITH PESTO, GORGONZOLA

Level of difficulty:
Preparation time: 20 mins
Number of hamburgers: 4

Type of meat

BEEF

BUNS
homemade or bought buns	4

PESTO
basil	240 g (9 oz)
garlic	2 cloves
pine nuts	1 tablespoon
olive oil	2 tablespoons
parmesan cheese, finely grated	50 g (1¾ oz/⅓ cup)

PATTIES
beef, minced (ground)	500 g (1 lb 2 oz)
sea salt	a few pinches

TOPPINGS
Gorgonzola cheese	100 g (3½ oz)
rocket (arugula)	a large handful

BUNS
Make the buns as described on page 14 or use ready-made buns.

PESTO
Pluck off the basil leaves and put them in a food processor with the garlic, pine nuts, olive oil and parmesan. Process everything together. Set aside 4 tablespoons of the pesto.

PATTIES
Combine the minced beef with three-quarters of the pesto and form 4 patties. Sprinkle with the sea salt.

TOPPINGS
Combine the rest of the pesto with the Gorgonzola.

COOKING THE PATTIES
Cook the patties in a hot frying pan over high heat, 3 minutes per side for rare patties.

ASSEMBLY
Cut the buns in half horizontally and toast them for 2 minutes under the grill (broiler). Spread the cut side of the bun heels and crowns with the 4 tablespoons of pesto. Put the patties and the pesto-Gorgonzola mix on top, then the rocket. Top with the crowns.

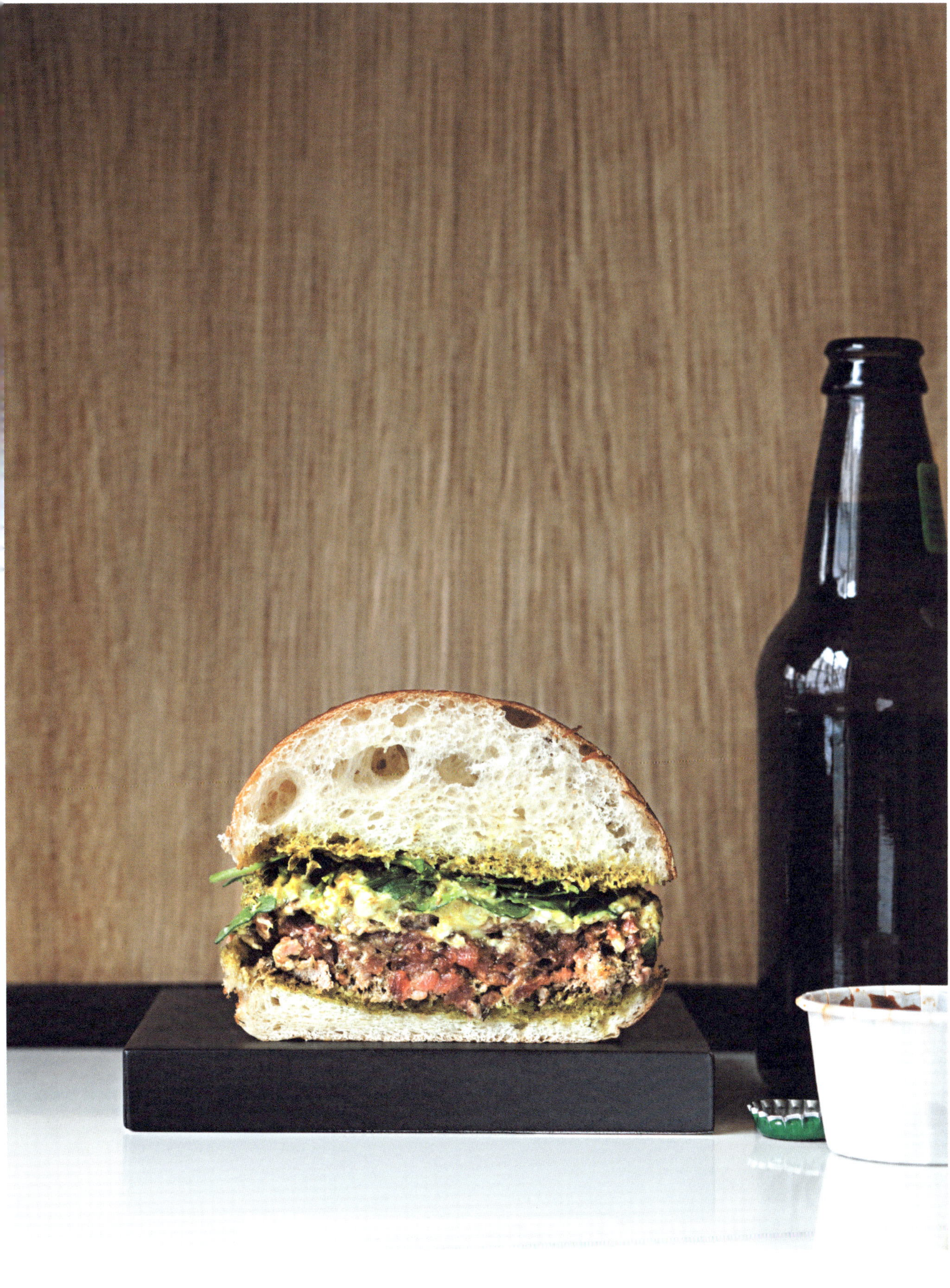

RECIPE NO. 36

CHORIZO

BEEF WITH CHORIZO, PAPRIKA

Level of difficulty:
Preparation time: 35 mins + 10 mins refrigeration time
Number of hamburgers: 4

Types of meat

BEEF + PIG

BUNS
homemade or bought buns	4

PATTIES
chorizo, finely chopped	150 g (5½ oz)
beef, minced (ground)	500 g (1 lb 2 oz)
paprika	1 teaspoon
sea salt	a few pinches

RELISH
tomato, finely diced	1
onion, thinly sliced	1
paprika	1 pinch
olive oil	2–3 tablespoons

TOPPINGS
rocket (arugula)	a large handful

BUNS
Make the buns as described on page 14 or use ready-made buns.

PATTIES
Add the chorizo to the minced beef with the paprika. Set aside in the refrigerator for 10 minutes. Form 4 patties and season with sea salt.

RELISH
Sauté the tomato and onion together in a frying pan with the paprika and olive oil for about 15 minutes.

COOKING THE PATTIES
Cook the patties in a hot frying pan over high heat, 3 minutes per side for rare patties.

ASSEMBLY
Cut the buns in half horizontally and toast them for 2 minutes under the grill (broiler). Spread the cut side of the bun crowns with a small amount of relish. On the bun heels spread half the remaining tomato-onion relish, the patties, the rest of the relish and the rocket. Finish with the crowns.

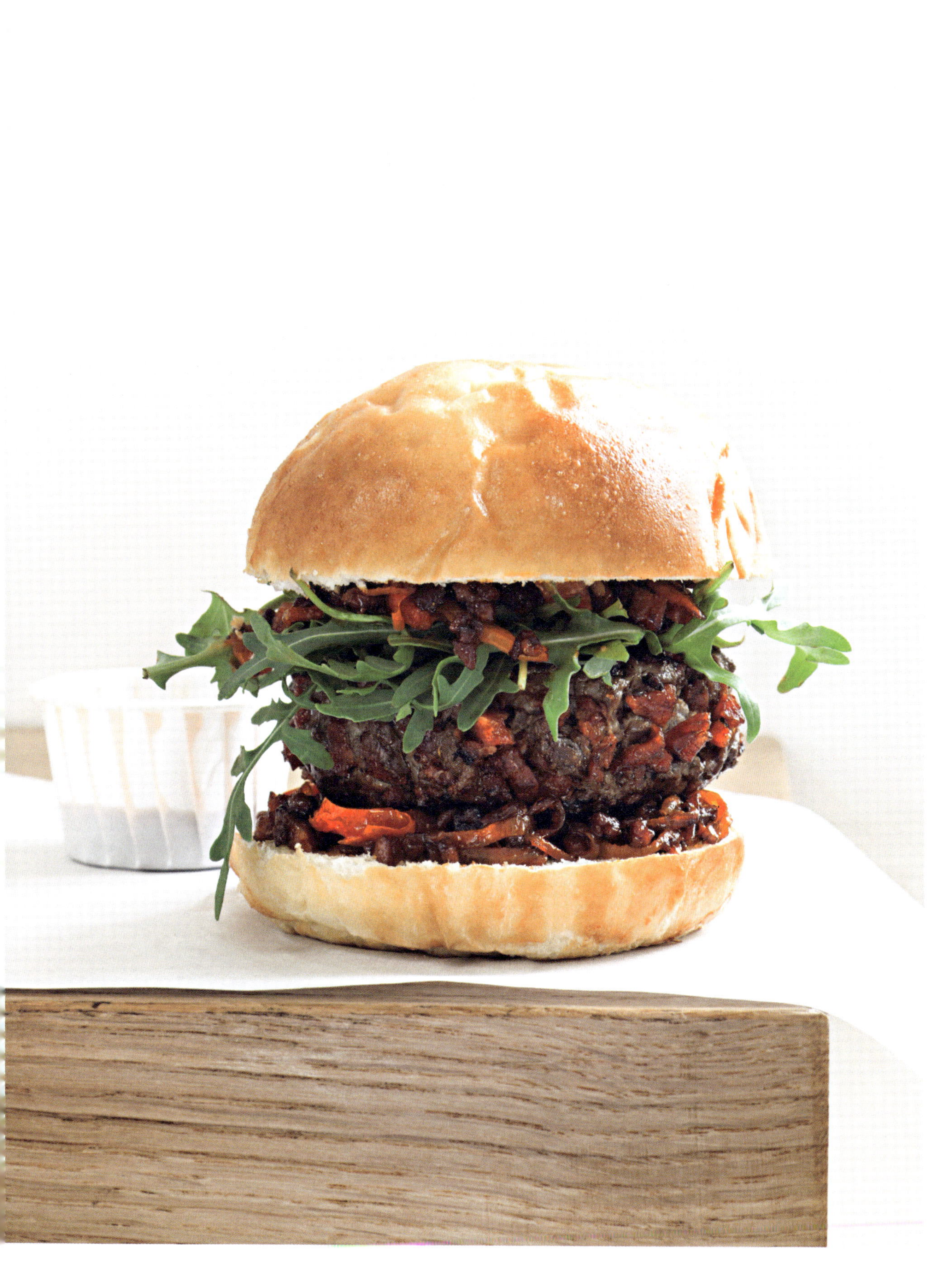

RECIPE NO. 37

HONEY

BEEF WITH PAPRIKA, HONEY

Level of difficulty:
Preparation time: 30 mins
Number of hamburgers: 4

Type of meat

BEEF

BUNS
| homemade or bought buns | 4 |

PATTIES
beef, minced (ground)	500 g (1 lb 2 oz)
sea salt	1 pinch
pepper	1 pinch
paprika	1 teaspoon
onion, diced	1
olive oil	1 drizzle

HONEY MAYONNAISE
egg yolk	1
mustard	1 teaspoon
honey	3 teaspoons
sunflower oil	500 ml (17 fl oz/2 cups)
toasted peanuts, chopped	2 teaspoons

TOPPINGS
| baby spinach | 45 g (1¾ oz/1 cup) |

BUNS
Make the buns as described on page 14 or use ready-made buns.

PATTIES
Form 4 patties from the minced beef.

HONEY MAYONNAISE
Put the egg yolk in a bowl with the mustard and honey. Using a whisk, combine gently and gradually add the sunflower oil in a thin stream. When the mayonnaise is ready add the peanuts to the preparation. Set aside in the refrigerator until needed.

COOKING THE PATTIES
Cook the patties in a frying pan over high heat for 5 minutes each side. Season them with salt, pepper and paprika and remove from the pan. Add the onion to the pan and brown in the olive oil for 4 minutes.

ASSEMBLY
Cut the buns in half horizontally and toast them for 2 minutes under the grill (broiler). Divide over the cut side of the bun heels the browned onions, the patties, then the mayonnaise and spinach leaves. Top with the crowns.

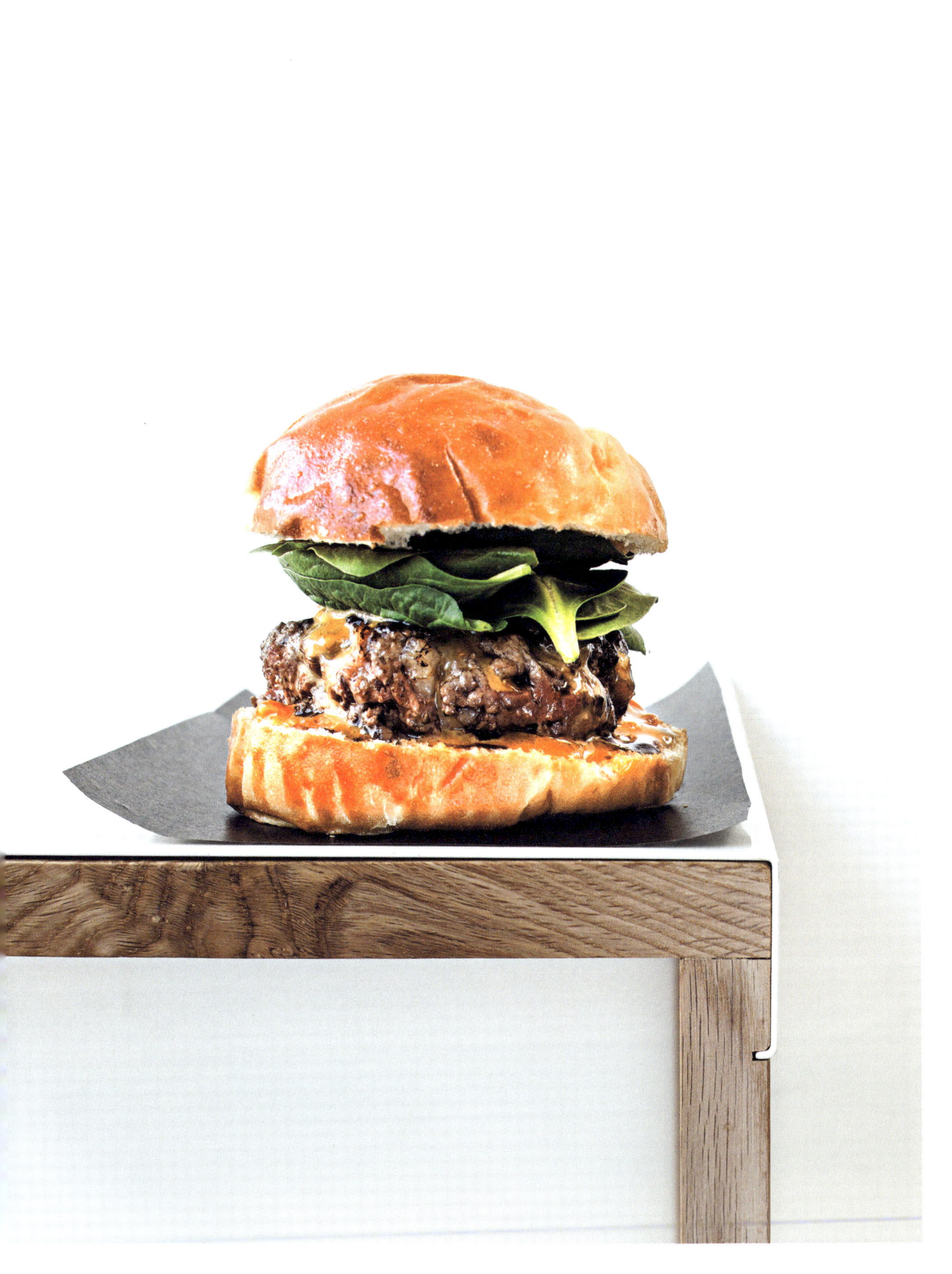

RECIPE NO. 38

ROSS
BEEF WITH FOIE GRAS, GINGERBREAD

Level of difficulty:
Preparation time: 35 mins
Number of hamburgers: 4

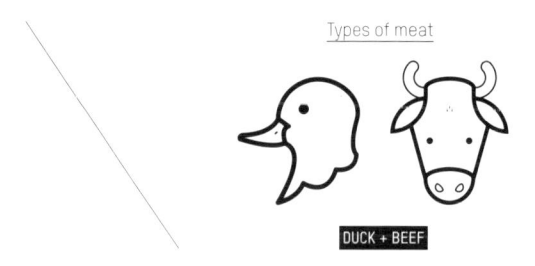

Types of meat

DUCK + BEEF

BUNS
homemade or bought buns	4

PATTIES
fresh foie gras	120 g (4¼ oz)
beef, minced (ground)	500 g (1 lb 2 oz)
sea salt	a few pinches

RELISH
brown onions, diced	3
olive oil	1 generous drizzle
sugar	100 g (3½ oz)

GINGERBREAD TUILES
olive oil	1 drizzle
gingerbread	4 thin slices

TOPPINGS
rocket (arugula)	a large handful

BUNS
Make the buns as described on page 14 or use ready-made buns.

PATTIES
Cut the foie gras into 4 thin slices (they must be round and smaller in diameter than the patties). Form 8 balls of minced beef of equal size, then flatten them. Put a slice of foie gras between 2 pieces of minced beef, then seal the edges well, making sure that the foie gras is not in contact with the outside. Repeat with the remaining minced beef and foie gras. Season the patties with the sea salt.

RELISH
Sauté the onions in a frying pan with the olive oil. Add the sugar and continue to cook until the onions caramelise.

GINGERBREAD TUILES
In a frying pan, heat the olive oil and sauté the slices of gingerbread so they crisp up, like tuile biscuits.

COOKING THE PATTIES
Cook the patties in a hot frying pan over high heat, 3 minutes per side for rare patties.

ASSEMBLY
Cut the buns in half horizontally and toast them for 2 minutes under the grill (broiler). Spread the onion relish over the cut side of the bun heels and add the foie gras patties. Top with rocket leaves and finally the gingerbread tuiles. Finish with the crowns.

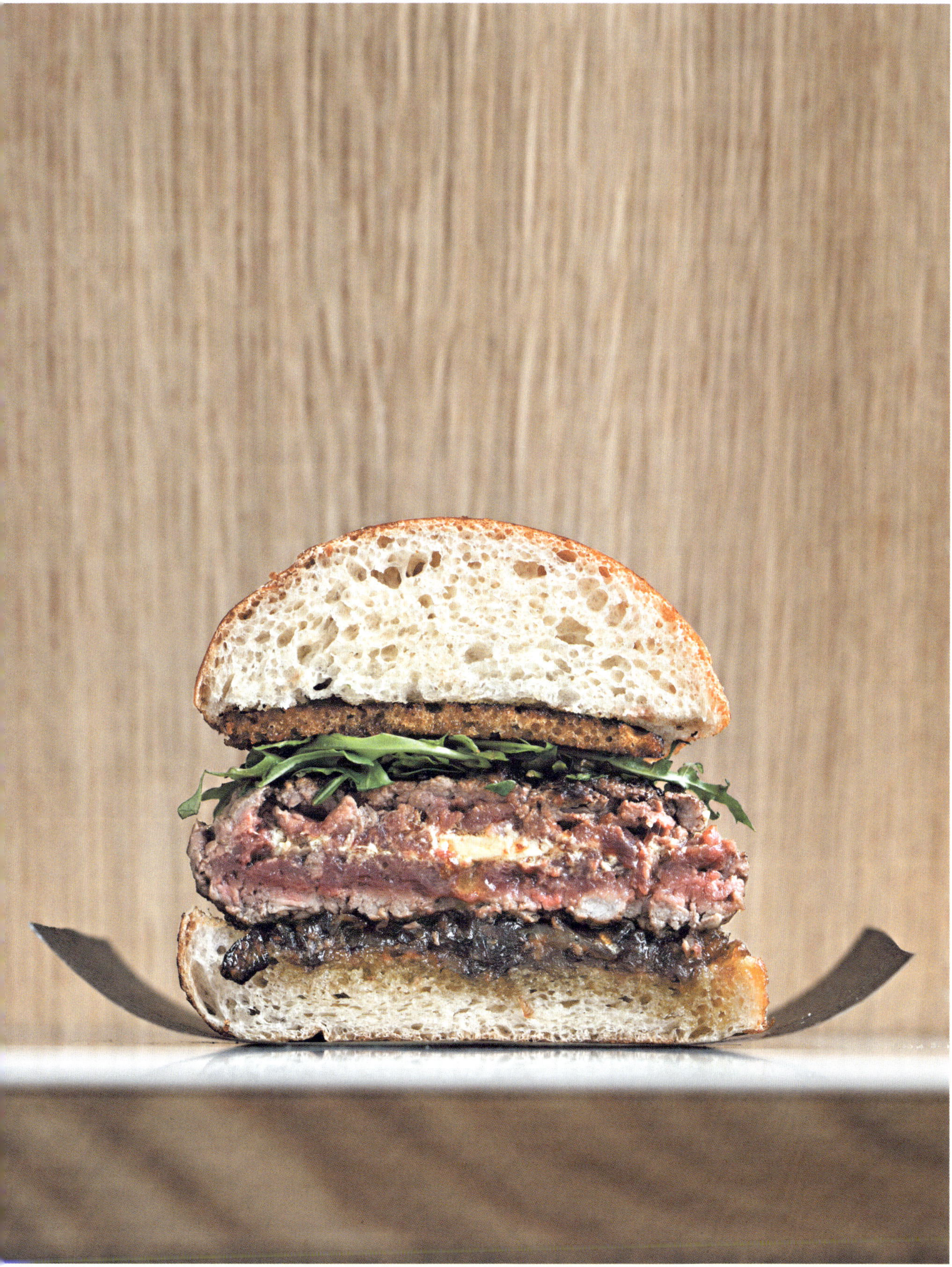

RECIPE NO. 39

MILK

LAMB WITH GARLIC, CONFITURE DE LAIT

Level of difficulty:
Preparation time: 20 mins + 10 mins refrigeration time + 1½–2 hours cooking time
Number of hamburgers: 4

Type of meat: LAMB

BUNS
homemade or bought buns	4

PATTIES
lamb, minced (ground)	500 g (1 lb 2 oz)
garlic, chopped	1 clove
sea salt	1 pinch
pepper	1 pinch

SAUCE
milk	500 ml (17 fl oz/2 cups)
sugar	250 g (9 oz)

TOPPINGS
baby spinach	45 g (1¾ oz/1 cup)

BUNS
Make the buns as described on page 14 or use ready-made buns.

PATTIES
Combine the minced lamb with the garlic. Form 4 patties and put them in the refrigerator for at least 10 minutes.

SAUCE
Pour the milk and sugar into a large saucepan. Bring to the boil then maintain at a simmer over low heat for 1 hour and 20 minutes, stirring about every 10 minutes. Cook until dark and jammy.

COOKING THE PATTIES
Once the milk jam is made, heat a frying pan over high heat. Season the patties with salt and pepper. When the pan is hot, add the patties and cook for 4 minutes on each side.

ASSEMBLY
Cut the buns in half horizontally and toast them for 2 minutes under the grill (broiler). Spread half of the milk jam on the cut side of the bun heels, put the lamb patties on top, add the remaining milk jam, then the spinach. Top with the crowns.

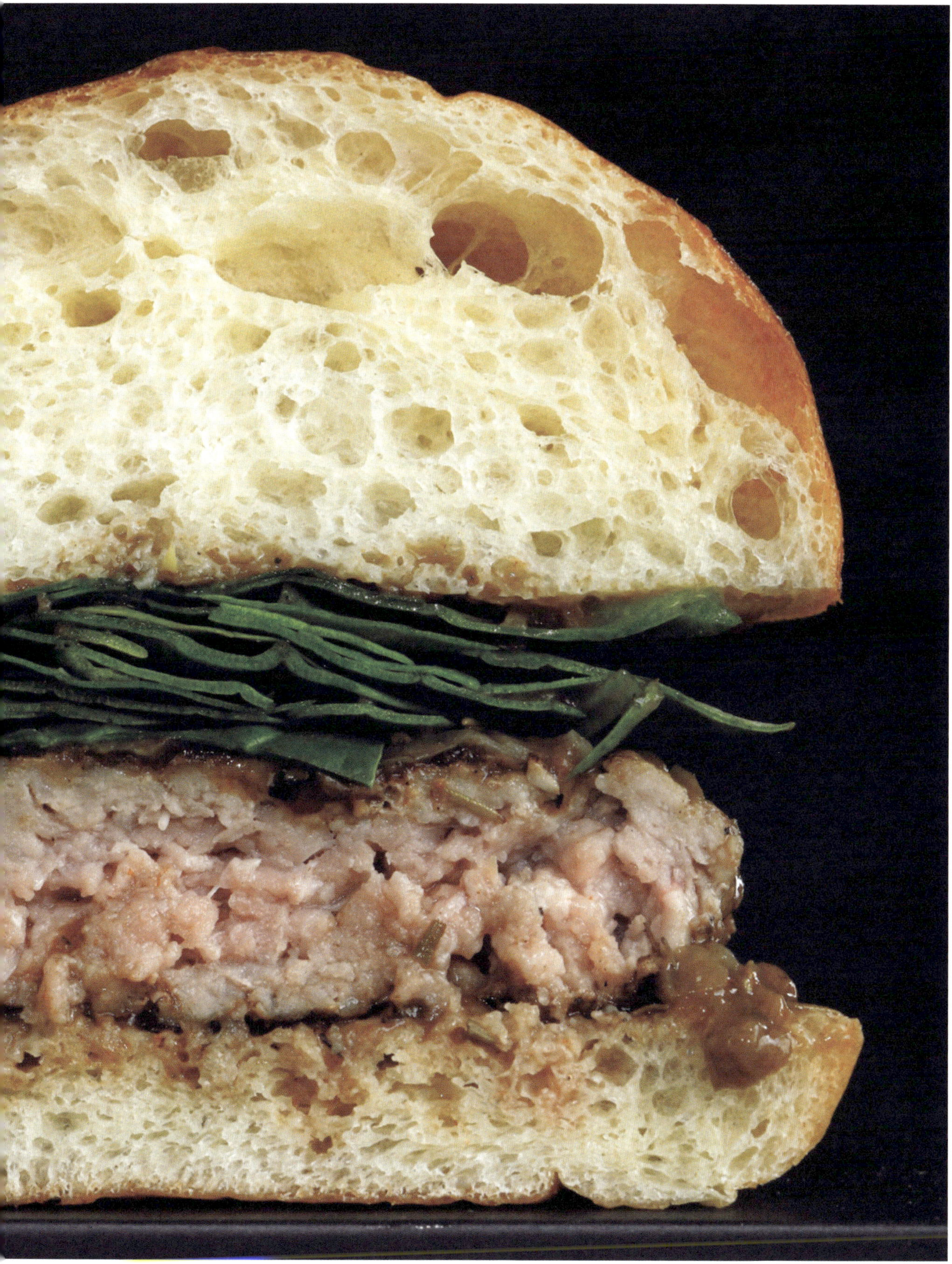

RECIPE NO. 40

TAJ

LAMB WITH PRUNES, ALMONDS

Level of difficulty:
Preparation time: 30 mins
Number of hamburgers: 4

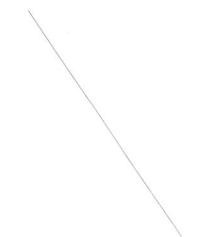

Type of meat

LAMB

BUNS
homemade or bought buns	4

PATTIES
lamb, minced (ground)	500 g (1 lb 2 oz)
almonds, chopped	3 teaspoons
prunes, chopped	40 g (1½ oz)
sea salt	a few pinches
olive oil	1 drizzle

SAUCE
raisins	50 g (1¾ oz)
rum	50 ml (1¾ fl oz)
olive oil	1 drizzle
onion, thinly sliced	1
thin (pouring) cream	200 ml (7 fl oz) + a little extra

TOPPINGS
rocket (arugula)	a large handful

BUNS
Make the buns as described on page 14 or use ready-made buns.

PATTIES
Combine the minced lamb, almonds and prunes and form 4 patties. Set aside in the refrigerator while you make the sauce.

SAUCE
Soak the raisins in the rum for 10 minutes, then drain, reserving the rum. Add the olive oil to a frying pan over high heat and sauté the onion. When it starts to brown, add the raisins. After 1 minute, deglaze with the reserved rum and flambé to remove the alcohol. Add the 200 ml (7 fl oz) of cream. Cook for a further 10 minutes over medium heat until the mixture is reduced. Allow to cool. Process the mixture in a food processor, adding the extra cream if it is too thick.

COOKING THE PATTIES
Season the patties with the sea salt and cook in the olive oil in a hot frying pan over high heat for 3 minutes on each side.

ASSEMBLY
Cut the buns in half horizontally and toast them for 2 minutes under the grill (broiler). Put the patties on the cut side of the bun heels, top with the onion-rum-raisin cream sauce, then the rocket leaves. Top with the crowns.

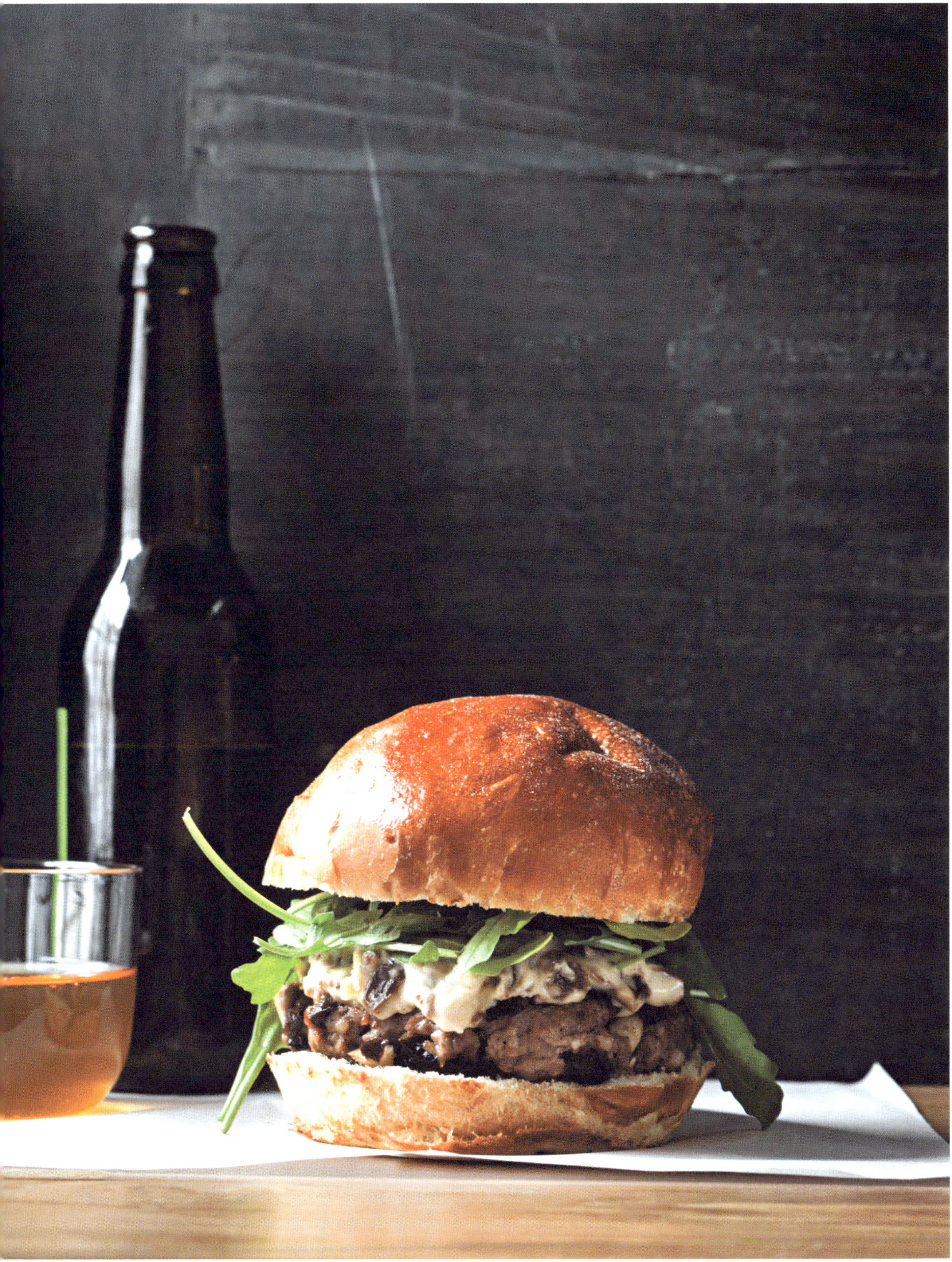

RECIPE NO. 41

MEX
PAPRIKA CHICKEN, AVOCADO

Level of difficulty:
Preparation time: 30 mins
Number of hamburgers: 4

Type of meat

CHICKEN

BUNS
homemade or bought buns	4

PATTIES
chicken breast fillet, diced	500 g (1 lb 2 oz)
paprika	1 pinch
sea salt	a few pinches
olive oil	1 drizzle
gouda cheese, cut into 4 slices	80 g (2¾ oz)

GUACAMOLE
avocados, mashed	2
Tabasco sauce	2 teaspoons
guacamole spice mix	1 tablespoon
salt	1 pinch
pepper	1 pinch

TOPPINGS
crème fraîche	20 g (¾ oz)
baby spinach	45 g (1¾ oz/1 cup)

BUNS
Make the buns as described on page 14 or use ready-made buns.

PATTIES
Combine the chicken and paprika. Make 4 patties, pressed together firmly, and season them with the sea salt.

GUACAMOLE
Combine the mashed avocados with the Tabasco sauce and the guacamole spice mix. Season with the salt and pepper and put in the refrigerator for at least 10 minutes.

COOKING THE PATTIES
Put the pattties in a hot frying pan with the olive oil. After 5 minutes, turn them over and put a slice of gouda cheese on each patty. Cover with a stainless steel bowl to melt the cheese and cook for a further 5 minutes.

ASSEMBLY
Cut the buns in half horizontally and toast them for 2 minutes under the grill (broiler). Spread the cut side of the bun heels with the crème fraîche and half the guacamole, add the patties with melted gouda and the baby spinach. Top with the crowns, spread with the remaining guacamole.

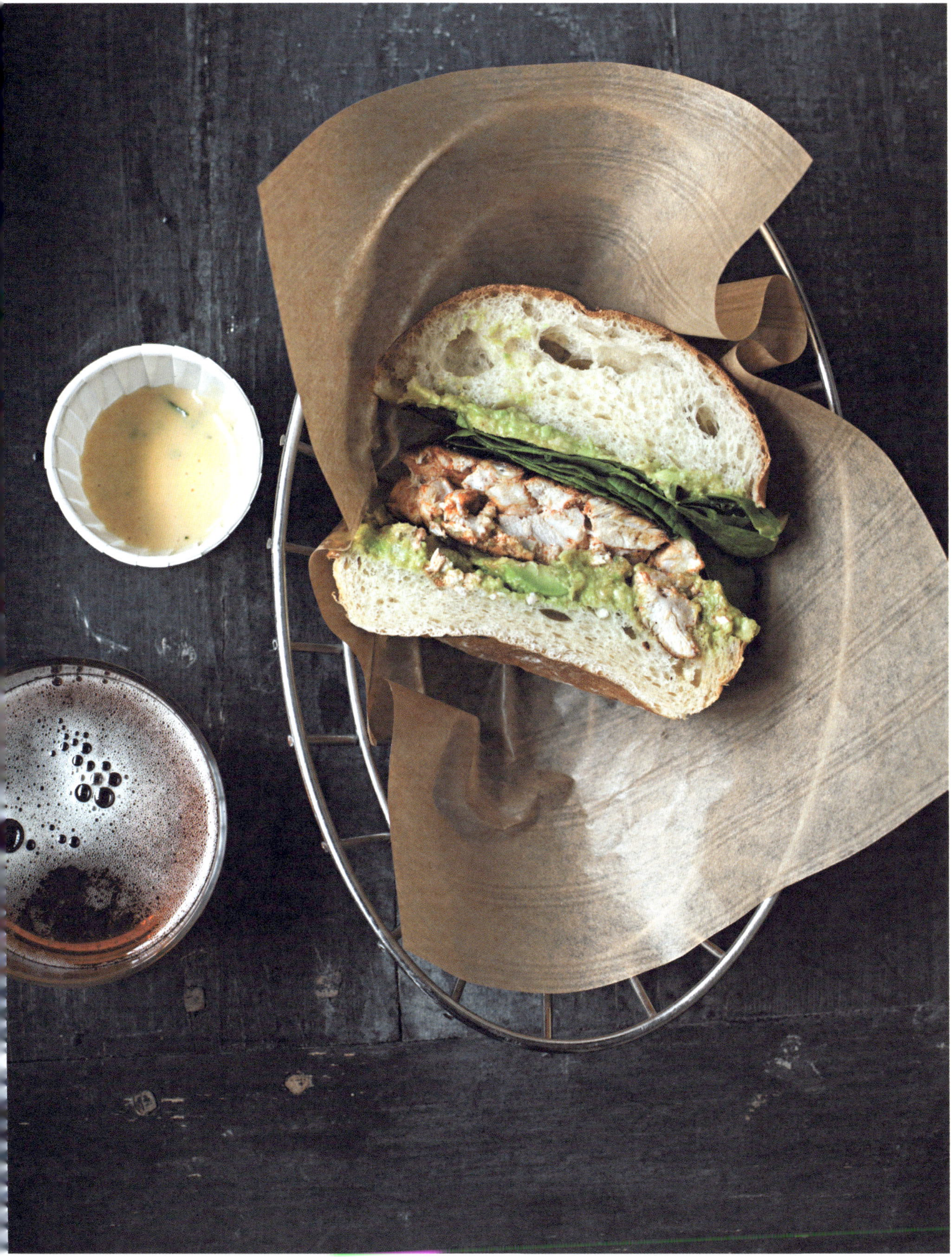

RECIPE NO. 42

BBQ
BARBECUE PIG

Type of meat: PIG

Level of difficulty:
Preparation time: 25 mins + 1 night marinating time
Number of hamburgers: 4

BUNS
homemade or bought buns	4

PATTIES
deboned pork loin chops, finely diced, fat retained	4
barbecue sauce (see page 26)	100 ml (3½ fl oz)
olive oil	1 drizzle

TOPPINGS
tomatoes, sliced	2
olive oil	1 drizzle
herbes de Provence	1 pinch
iceberg lettuce, shredded	¼

BUNS
Make the buns as described on page 14 or use ready-made buns.

PATTIES
Marinate the pork overnight in the barbecue sauce (set a little aside of the sauce for the assembly stage). Remove the pork from the marinade, squeezing out excess liquid, and shape it into 4 patties.

TOPPINGS
Brown the tomatoes in a frying pan with the olive oil over high heat, adding the herbes de Provence.

COOKING THE PATTIES
Preheat the oven to 170°C (325°F/Gas 3). Heat a drizzle of olive oil in a frying pan over high heat. Sear the patties in the oil for 2 minutes on each side then put the patties on a lightly greased baking tray and transfer to the preheated oven for 10 minutes.

ASSEMBLY
Cut the buns in half horizontally and toast them for 2 minutes under the grill (broiler). Spread the cut side of the bun heels with the reserved barbecue sauce, divide half the fried tomatoes between them, add the patties, then the rest of the tomatoes and the shredded lettuce. Top with the crowns.

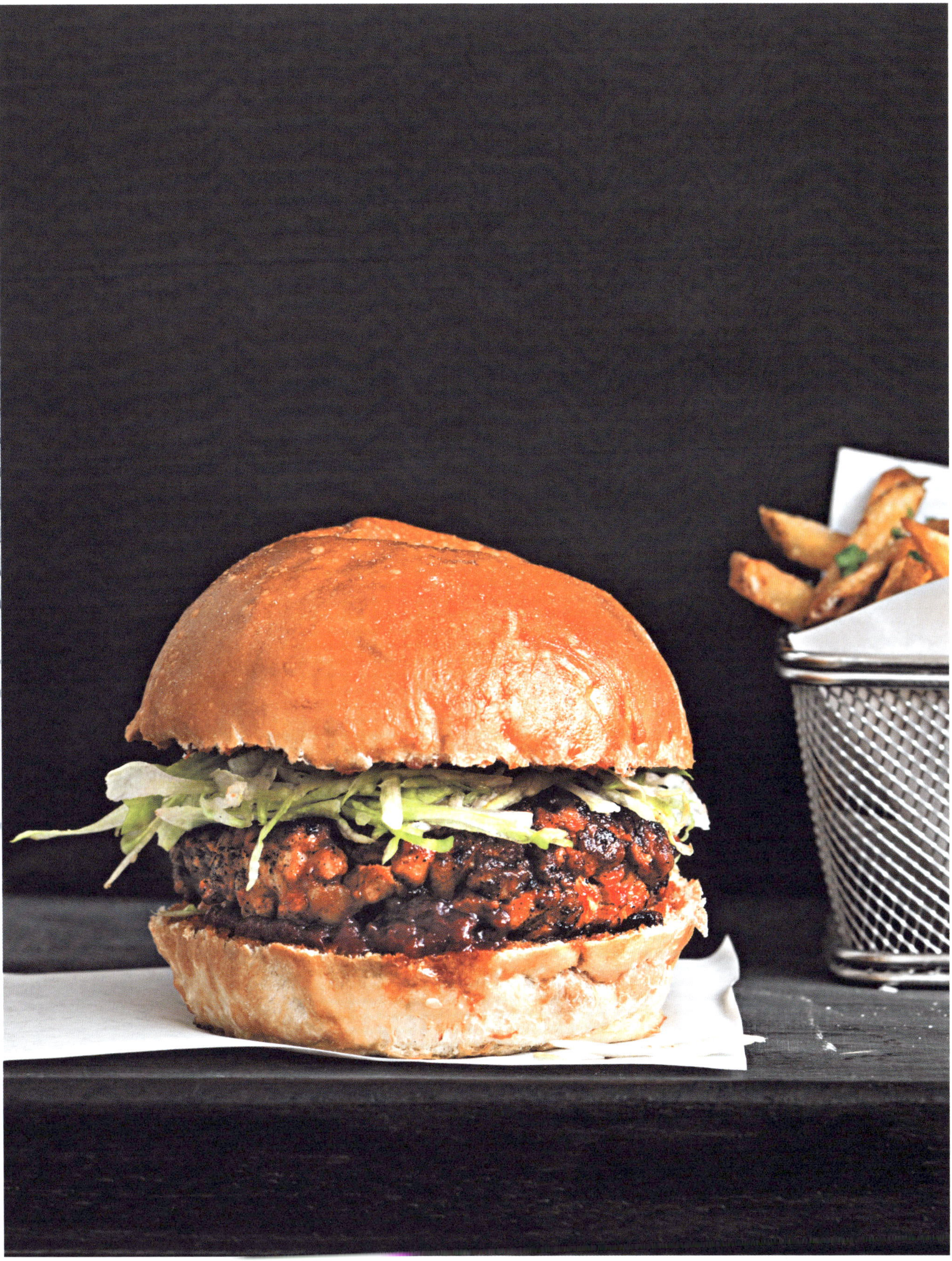

RECIPE NO. 43

CREO

SPICY CRAB, MAYO

Level of difficulty:
Preparation time: 35 mins
Number of hamburgers: 4

Type of meat

CRAB

BUNS

homemade or bought buns	4

PATTIES

crabmeat (tinned or fresh)	450 g (1 lb)
French shallots, finely chopped	3
egg	1
worcestershire sauce	1 teaspoon
mustard powder	¾ teaspoon
cayenne pepper	½ teaspoon
salt	1 pinch
mayonnaise	60 g (2¼ oz/¼ cup)
dry breadcrumbs	180 g (6½ oz)
vegetable oil	185 ml (6 fl oz/¾ cup)

RELISH

olive oil	a drizzle
French shallots, finely chopped	6
sugar	50 g (1¾ oz)
water	1 tablespoon

TOPPINGS

baby spinach	45 g (1¾ oz/1 cup)

BUNS

Make the buns as described on page 14 or use ready-made buns.

PATTIES

Combine the crabmeat with the shallots, egg, worcestershire sauce, mustard powder, cayenne pepper, salt and mayonnaise, reserving 1 tablespoon of the mayonnaise for assembly. Add 125 g (4½ oz) of the breadcrumbs and combine until the mixture is even. Form 4 patties with this mixture (don't worry if it seems soft). Put the remaining breadcrumbs on a plate. Dip the patties in the breadcrumbs.

RELISH

Put the olive oil in a frying pan. Sauté the shallots in the oil over low heat, then, incorporating the sugar and water gradually and stirring regularly, cook for about 15-20 minutes, or until jammy.

COOKING THE PATTIES

Pour the vegetable oil in a deep frying pan over medium heat until it is just sizzling. Cook the patties for 3 minutes on each side. Transfer them to paper towels.

ASSEMBLY

Cut the buns in half horizontally and toast them for 2 minutes under the grill (broiler). Spread the cut side of the bun heels with the reserved mayonnaise and add half the relish, the patties, the rest of the relish and a few spinach leaves. Top with the crowns.

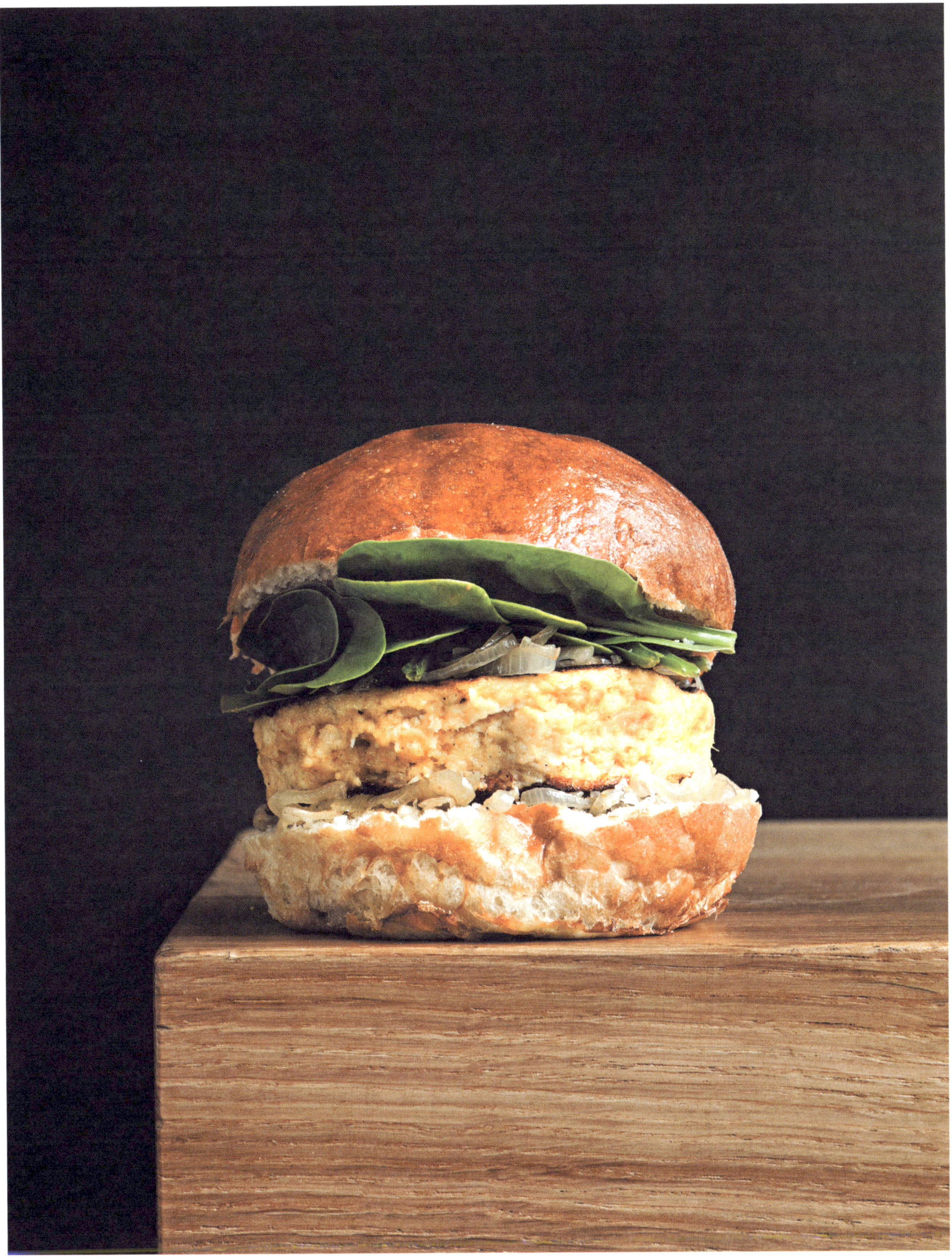

3/

VEGGIE / 100% VEGETABLE

VEGGIE
LEGUMES
100%

RECIPE NO. 44

QUINOA
THE CLASSIC WITH GRAINS

Level of difficulty: 🍔🍔
Preparation time: 35 mins + 10 mins refrigeration time
Number of hamburgers: 4

Type of vegetable

GRAINS

BUNS
homemade or bought buns	4

SAUCE
dijon mustard	100 g (3½ oz)
honey	2 tablespoons
cider vinegar	2 teaspoons
celery salt	2 pinches
white pepper	2 pinches

PATTIES
raw beetroot (beet), peeled, scrubbed and sliced	1
quinoa	200 g (7 oz/1 cup)
burghul (bulgur)	125 g (4½ oz)
French shallots	3
dry breadcrumbs	100 g (3½ oz)
salt	1 pinch
pepper	1 pinch
vegetable oil	1 drizzle

TOPPINGS
rocket	45 g (1¾ oz/1 cup)

BUNS
Make the buns as described on page 14 or use ready-made buns.

SAUCE
Combine the mustard with the honey, cider vinegar, celery salt and white pepper.

PATTIES
Steam the beetroot slices for 5–7 minutes, then marinate in half the sauce, reserving the other half to spread on the buns. Cook the quinoa and burghul according to the packet instructions, then put them in a food processor bowl with the shallots. Coarsely process in short pulses. Add the beetroot and pulse to roughly combine. Form 4 patties from the processed mixture and put in the refrigerator for at least 10 minutes. Combine the breadcrumbs, salt and pepper in a bowl. Coat each patty with this mixture.

COOKING THE PATTIES
Pour a layer of vegetable oil on the base of a deep saucepan (approximately 1.5 cm/⅝ inch deep), or use a deep-fryer if you have one. Over high heat, when the oil is quite hot, cook the crumbed patties for about 8 minutes in total.

ASSEMBLY
Cut the buns in half horizontally and toast them for 2 minutes under the grill (broiler). Spread the cut side of the bun heels with half of the honey-mustard sauce and top with the vegetable patties, a few leaves of rocket, the remaining honey-mustard sauce and the crowns.

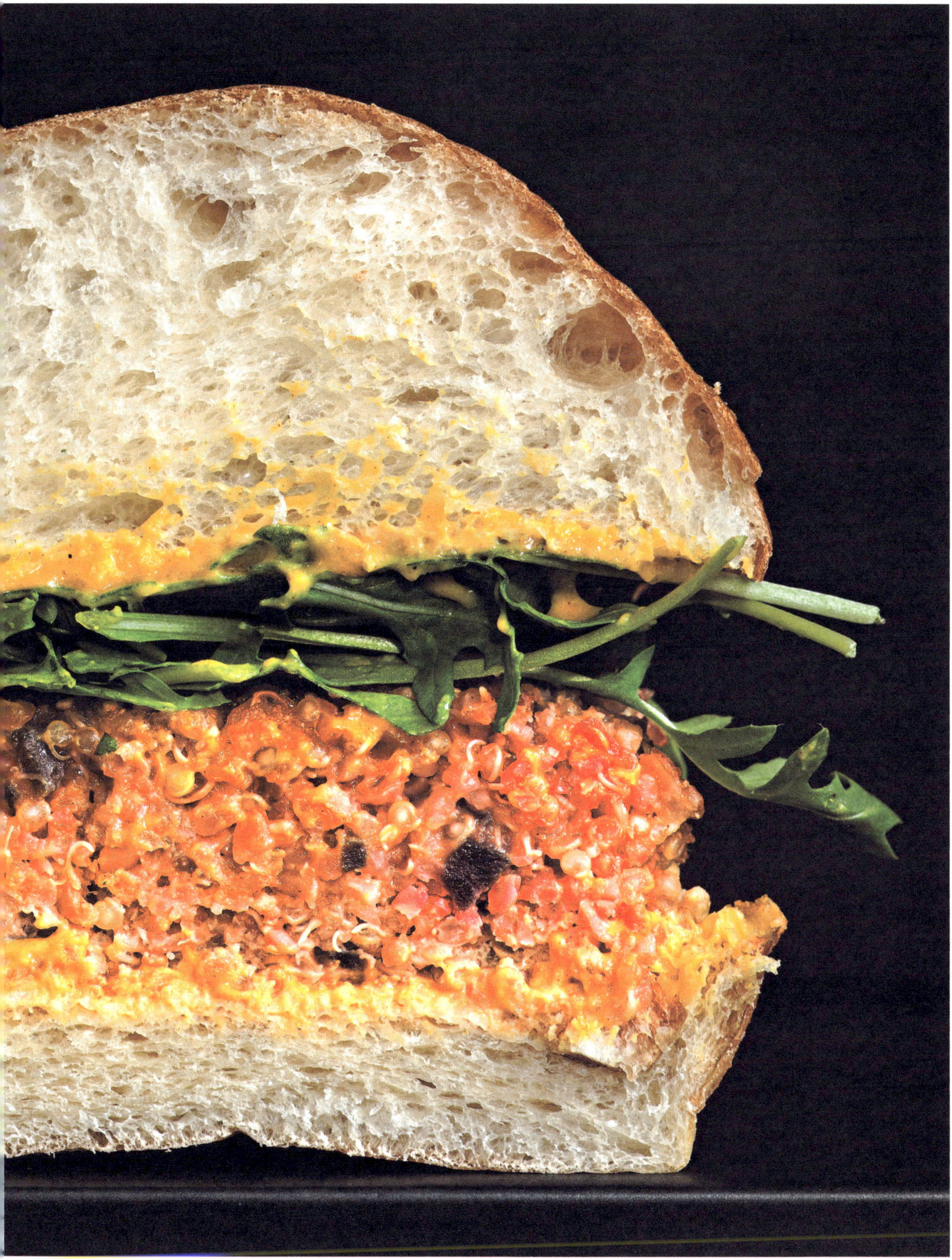

RECIPE NO. 45

GREENIE
VEGETABLE TOMATO SAUCE

Level of difficulty: ●●
Preparation time: 35 mins
Number of hamburgers: 4

Type of vegetable

FRESH VEGETABLES

BUNS
homemade or bought buns	4

PATTIES
potatoes	3
carrots	2
green beans	50 g (1¾ oz)
zucchini (courgettes)	3
garlic	2 cloves
plain (all-purpose) flour	40 g (1½ oz)
dry breadcrumbs	80 g (2¾ oz/⅔ cup)
olive oil	for frying

TOMATO SAUCE
tomato, diced	1
onion, diced	½
olive oil	1 drizzle
salt	1 pinch
pepper	1 pinch

TOPPINGS
iceberg lettuce, shredded	¼

BUNS
Make the buns as described on page 14 or use ready-made buns.

PATTIES
Prepare the vegetables: peel the potatoes and carrots, then cut all the vegetables into pieces. Add the potato, carrot and garlic to boiling salted water and cook for 15 minutes or until softened, adding the beans and zucchini after 5 minutes. Drain, then mash them and allow the mixture to cool for a few minutes. Add the flour and form 4 patties. Season well.

TOMATO SAUCE
Cook the tomato and onion for 10 minutes over low heat in a saucepan with a little olive oil until you have a tomato sauce. Season with salt and pepper.

COOKING THE PATTIES
Coat the patties with the breadcrumbs and brown them in a frying pan in olive oil for 5 minutes on each side.

ASSEMBLY
Cut the buns in half horizontally and toast them for 2 minutes under the grill (broiler). Spread the cut side of the bun heels and crowns with the tomato sauce. On the heels add the patties and the lettuce. Top with the crowns.

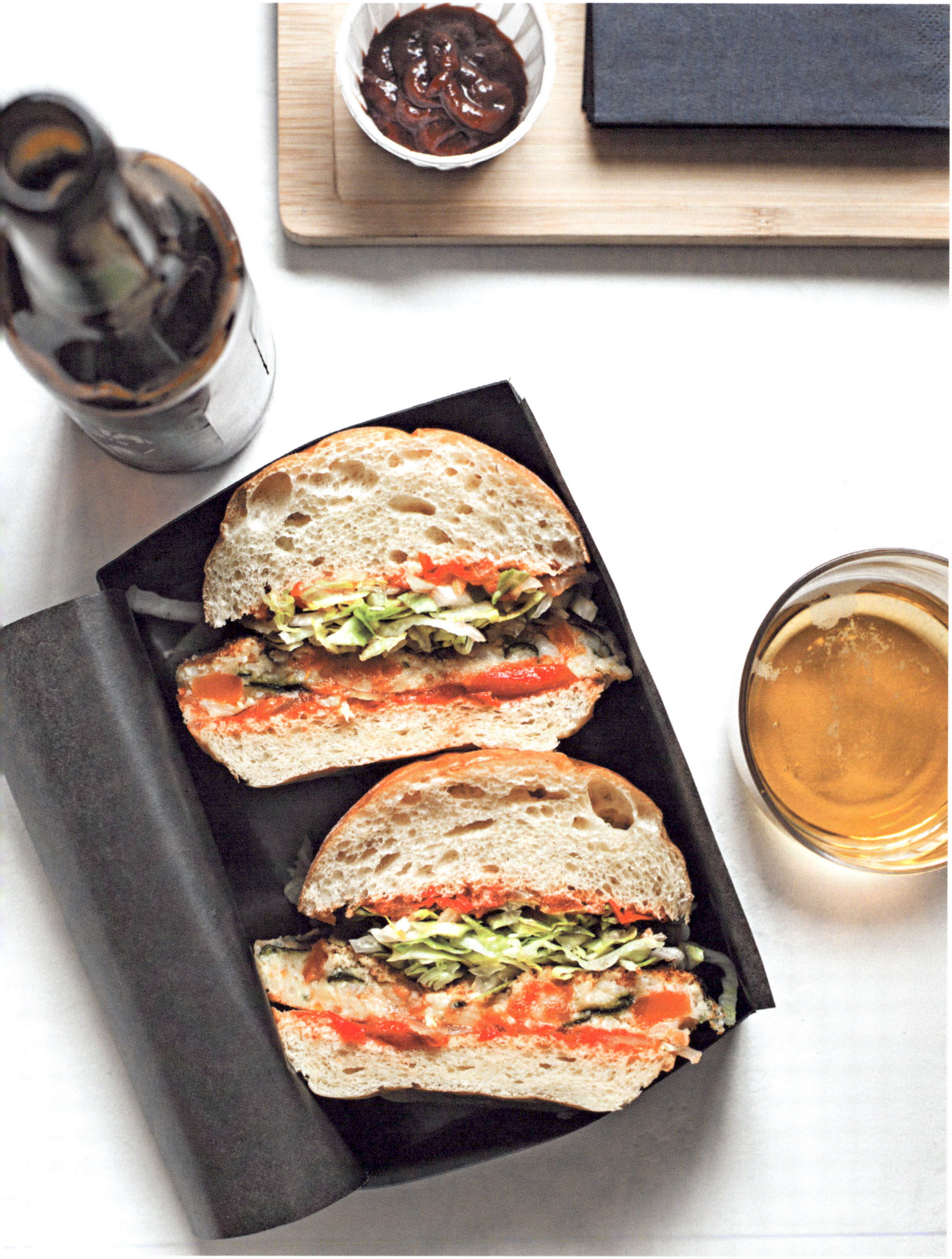

RECIPE NO. 46

BEANS
BEANS, LENTILS

Level of difficulty:
Preparation time: 45 minutes + soaking time for beans and lentils
Number of hamburgers: 4

Type of vegetable

PULSES

BUNS
homemade or bought buns	4

PATTIES
white beans	150 g (5½ oz)
brown lentils	100 g (3½ oz)
salt	1 pinch
onion, diced	1
olive oil	1 drizzle
egg	1
sea salt	a few pinches

SAUCE
ricotta	100 g (3½ oz)
parsley, chopped	6 leaves

TOPPINGS
mesclun salad	a large handful

BUNS
Make the buns as described on page 14 or use ready-made buns.

PATTIES
Soak the beans and lentils for 1 hour before cooking. Cook in separate saucepans in salted water for about 30–40 minutes, or until soft. Drain, then set aside to cool. Sauté the onion in a frying pan with a little olive oil. Add the onion to the cooled lentils and beans in a food processor bowl and pulse until well combined. Add the egg and process further. Form 4 patties and season them with the sea salt.

SAUCE
Combine the ricotta with the parsley.

COOKING THE PATTIES
Put the patties for on a lightly greased baking tray and cook them for 10 minutes in an oven preheated to 170°C (325°F/Gas 3).

ASSEMBLY
Cut the buns in half horizontally and toast them for 2 minutes under the grill (broiler). Spread the cut side of the bun heels with the ricotta-parsley sauce, top with the patties and the mesclun, then cap off with the crowns.

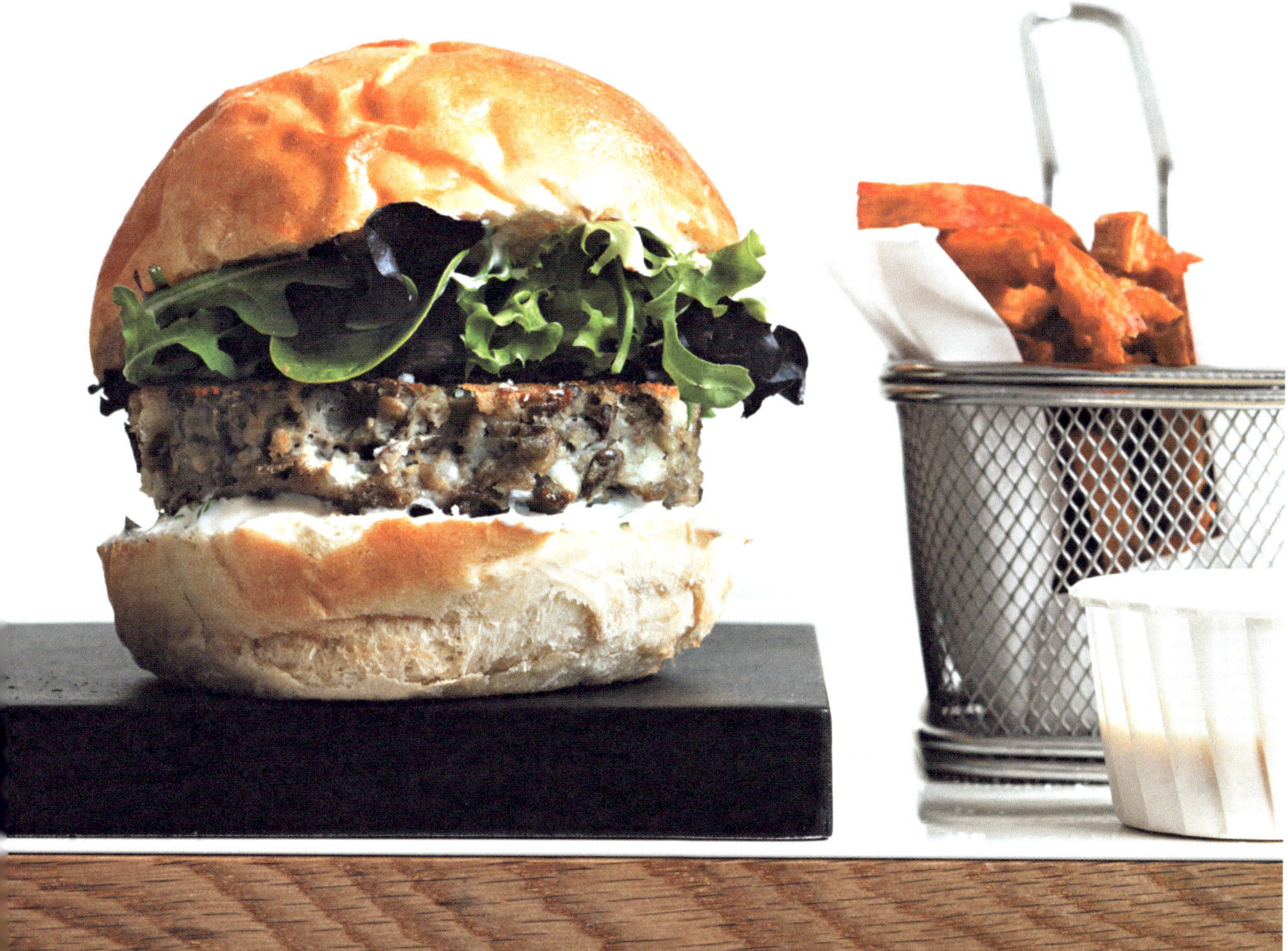

RECIPE NO. 47

BURG

BURGHUL, WALNUTS, CUMIN

Level of difficulty:
Preparation time: 45 mins + 10 mins refrigeration time
Number of hamburgers: 4

Type of vegetable

GRAINS

BUNS
homemade or bought buns	4

PATTIES
onion, finely chopped	1
olive oil	2 tablespoons
burghul (bulgur)	80 g (2¾ oz)
water	230 ml (7¾ fl oz)
tinned white beans, drained and rinsed	250 g (9 oz)
soy sauce	30 ml (1 fl oz)
walnuts	75 g (2¾ oz)
garlic, finely chopped	2 cloves
fresh coriander (cilantro) leaves	45 g (1¾ oz)
ground cumin	¼ teaspoon
cayenne pepper	¼ teaspoon
salt	1 pinch
pepper	1 pinch

SAUCE
mayonnaise	60 g (2¼ oz/¼ cup)
lemon juice	1 teaspoon
lemon zest	1 teaspoon

TOPPINGS
oxheart tomato	1
olive oil	2–3 tablespoons
herbes de Provence	1 pinch
rocket (arugula)	a large handful

BUNS
Make the buns as described on page 14 or use ready-made buns.

PATTIES
Lightly brown half the onion for 5–7 minutes with a drizzle of olive oil over low heat in a saucepan. Add the burghul and water and cook for 15–20 minutes, covered, over low heat until the water has been completely absorbed. Pour the burghul mixture into a food processor bowl, then add the white beans and soy sauce. Process the mixture, adding the walnuts, garlic, coriander, cumin, cayenne pepper, salt, pepper and the remaining onion to make an even mixture. Work the mixture in short pulses, taking care to not over-process. Form 4 patties and put them in the refrigerator for at least 10 minutes.

SAUCE
Combine the mayonnaise with the lemon juice and zest.

TOPPINGS
Cut the tomato into 4 rounds. Cover them with olive oil and sprinkle with herbes de Provence. Cook them in a hot frying pan for 5 minutes, turning them halfway through the cooking time.

COOKING THE PATTIES
Brush both sides of the patties with olive oil. Cook the patties for about 5–6 minutes each side in a hot frying pan over high heat.

ASSEMBLY
Cut the buns in half horizontally and toast them for 2 minutes under the grill (broiler). Spread the cut side of the bun heels with the sauce, add the cooked tomato slices, the patties, a few rocket leaves, then the crowns.

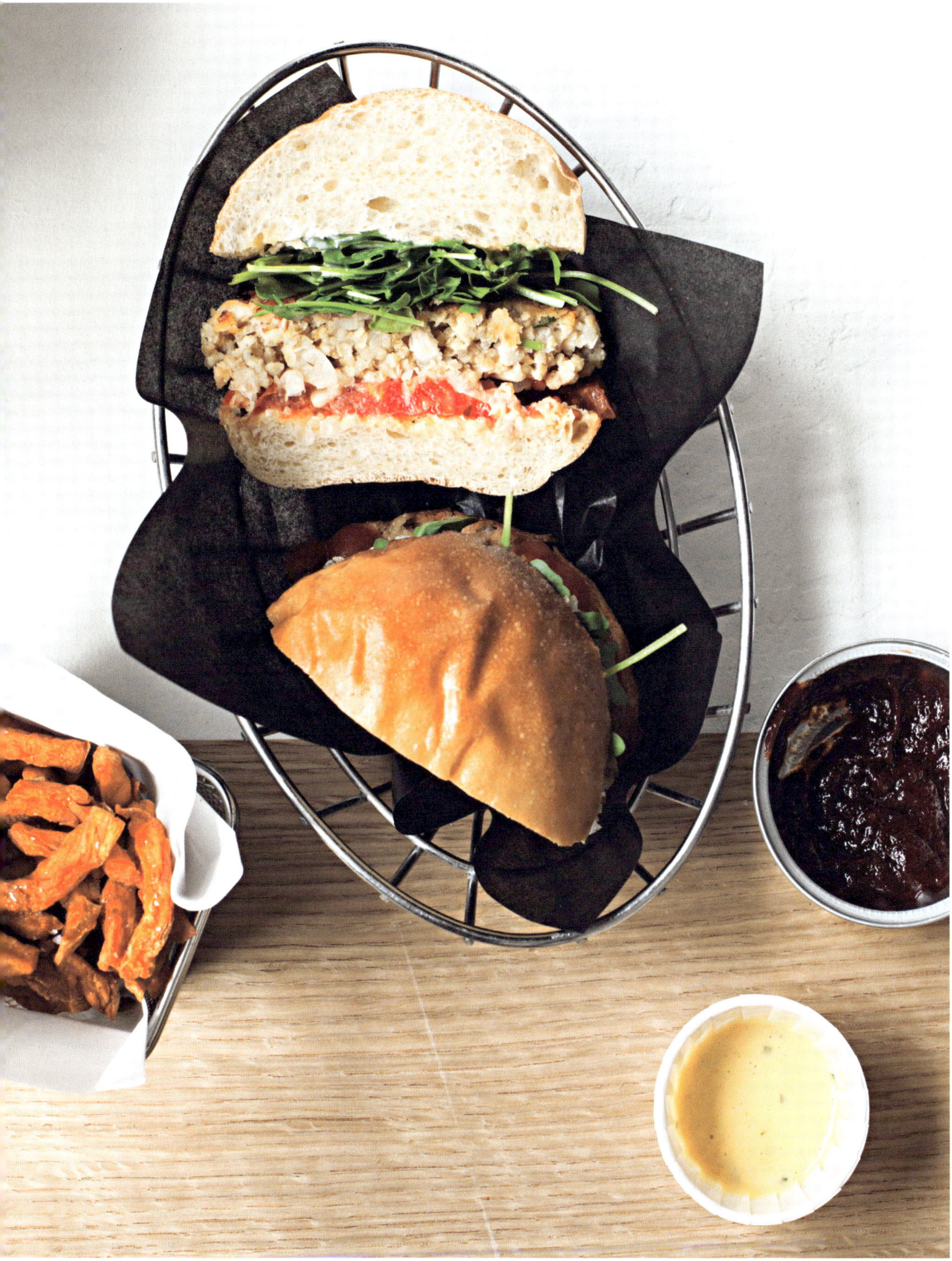

RECIPE NO. 48

TOFU

TOFU, ZUCCHINI

Level of difficulty: ●●
Preparation time: 30 mins
Number of hamburgers: 4

Type of vegetable

FRESH VEGETABLES + GRAINS

BUNS
homemade or bought buns	4

PATTIES
zucchini (courgettes), sliced into rounds	3
onion, diced	½
olive oil	1 drizzle
tofu	2 squares
sea salt	a few pinches

TOMATO SAUCE
tomato, diced	1
onion, diced	½
olive oil	1 drizzle

TOPPINGS
mesclun salad	a large handful

BUNS
Make the buns as described on page 14 or use ready-made buns.

PATTIES
Sauté the zucchini and onion in a frying pan with the olive oil until softened. Chop the tofu in a food processor. When the zucchini mixture is cooked, combine it with the tofu and work it together well to make a smooth mixture (a quicker method is to process it roughly in a food processor). Form 4 patties and season them with the sea salt.

TOMATO SAUCE
Soften the tomato and onion in a small saucepan over low heat with a little olive oil, until you have a tomato sauce.

COOKING THE PATTIES
Put the patties on a lightly greased baking tray and cook them for 10 minutes in an oven preheated to 180°C (350°F/Gas 4).

ASSEMBLY
Cut the buns in half horizontally and toast them for 2 minutes under the grill (broiler). Top the cut side of the bun heels with the tomato sauce, add the zucchini-tofu patties and the mesclun, then cap off with the crowns.

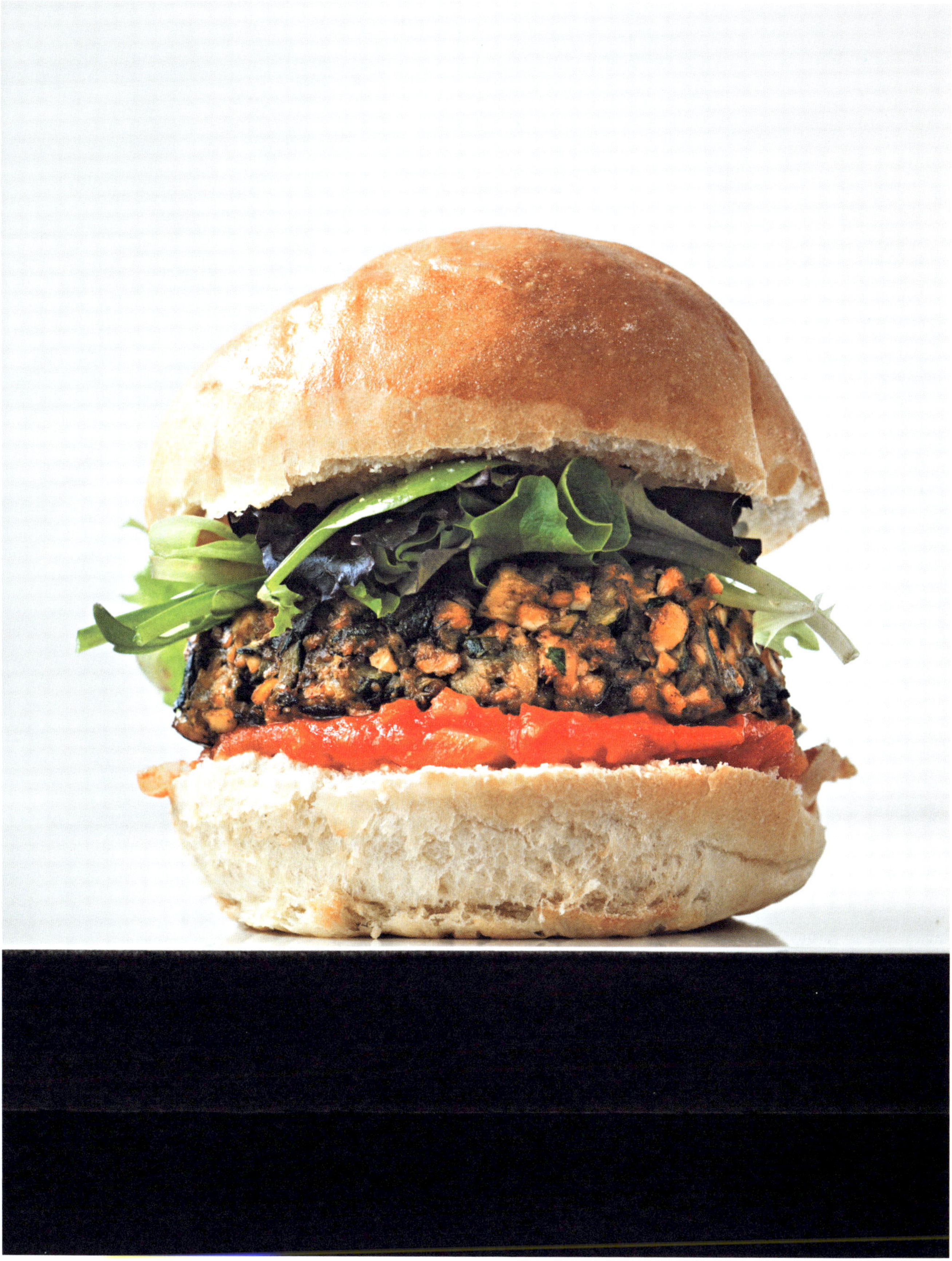

RECIPE NO. 49

CHILL
CHILLI VEGGIE

Level of difficulty: ●●●
Preparation time: 30 mins
Number of hamburgers: 4

Type of vegetable

GRAINS + PULSES

BUNS
| homemade or bought buns | 4 |

PATTIES
tinned red kidney beans, drained and rinsed	250 g (9 oz)
tinned corn kernels, drained	100 g (3½ oz)
plain (all-purpose) flour	150 g (5½ oz/1 cup)
eggs, beaten	3
cayenne pepper	1 teaspoon

SAUCE
orange blossom honey	3 teaspoons
wholegrain mustard	2 tablespoons
olive oil	1 tablespoon

TOPPINGS
| mâche | 1 cup |

BUNS
Make the buns as described on page 14 or use ready-made buns.

PATTIES
Set aside 1 handful of red kidney beans and in a food processor coarsely process the rest. Add the corn, the whole beans, flour and beaten eggs. Sprinkle with cayenne pepper and salt then combine the mixture. Place 4 ring moulds on a lightly greased baking tray and add the batter to form the patties.

SAUCE
Combine the honey and mustard. Add the olive oil and whisk vigorously.

COOKING THE PATTIES
Cook the patties for 14-15 minutes in an oven preheated to 180°C (350°F/Gas 4).

ASSEMBLY
Cut the buns in half horizontally and toast them for 2 minutes under the grill (broiler). Spread the cut side of the bun heels and crowns with the honey-mustard sauce. Put the patties on the bun heels, add the mâche and cap with the crowns.

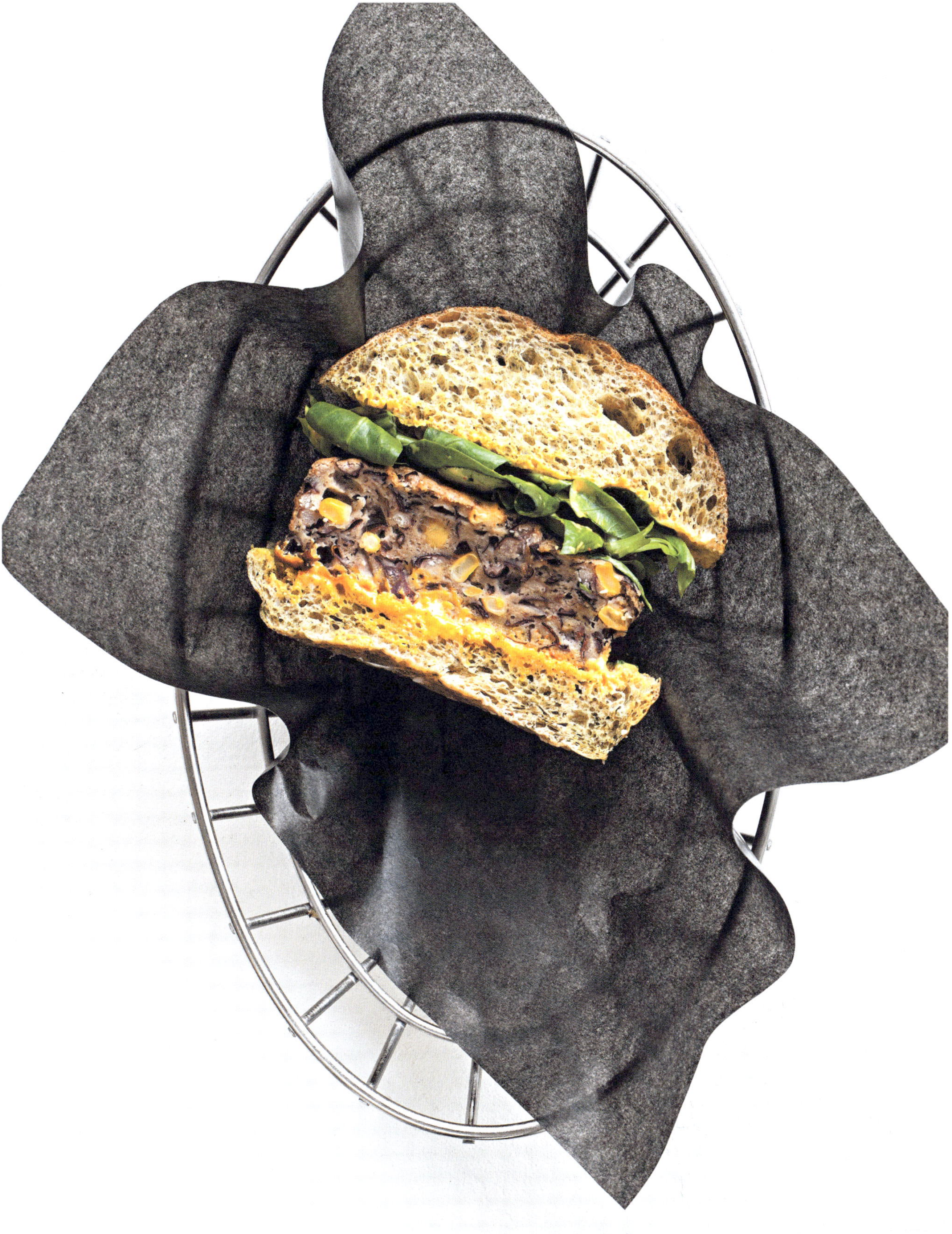

4

AT THE CUTTING EDGE / RECIPES FROM THE CHEF

RECIPES FROM THE CHEF

AT THE CUTTING EDGE

RECIPE NO. 50

MEAT
THE BEST OF THE HAMBURGER

Level of difficulty:
Preparation time: 30 mins + 2 hours refrigeration time
Number of hamburgers: 4

Type of meat

BEEF

BUNS
homemade or bought buns 4

PATTIES
beef **500 g (1 lb 2 oz) (⅓ fillet + ⅔ blade)**
salt .... **4 pinches**
salted butter .... **1 small knob**
freshly ground black pepper .... **4 pinches**

TOPPINGS
baby spinach .... **45 g (1¾ oz/1 cup)**

BUNS
Make the buns as described on page 14 or use ready-made buns.

PATTIES
Using a knife, cut the fillet into thin strips, in the direction of the grain. Then cut across the strips to make small cubes. Do the same with the blade beef and combine with the fillet in a small mixing bowl. Wet fingers in a bowl of lukewarm water. Form 4 patties, pressing the meat firmly so the pieces hold together during cooking. Put 1 pinch of salt on each patty. Set them aside in the refrigerator for at least 2 hours.

COOKING THE PATTIES
Put a small knob of butter into a frying pan over high heat. Start cooking the patties before the butter is completely melted. Cook them for 3 minutes on each side, for rare patties. After turning them and cooking for a further 3 minutes, add the freshly ground black pepper on top.

ASSEMBLY
Cut the buns in half horizontally and toast them for 2 minutes under the grill (broiler). Put the patties on the cut side of the bun heels, then top with the spinach and finally the crowns.

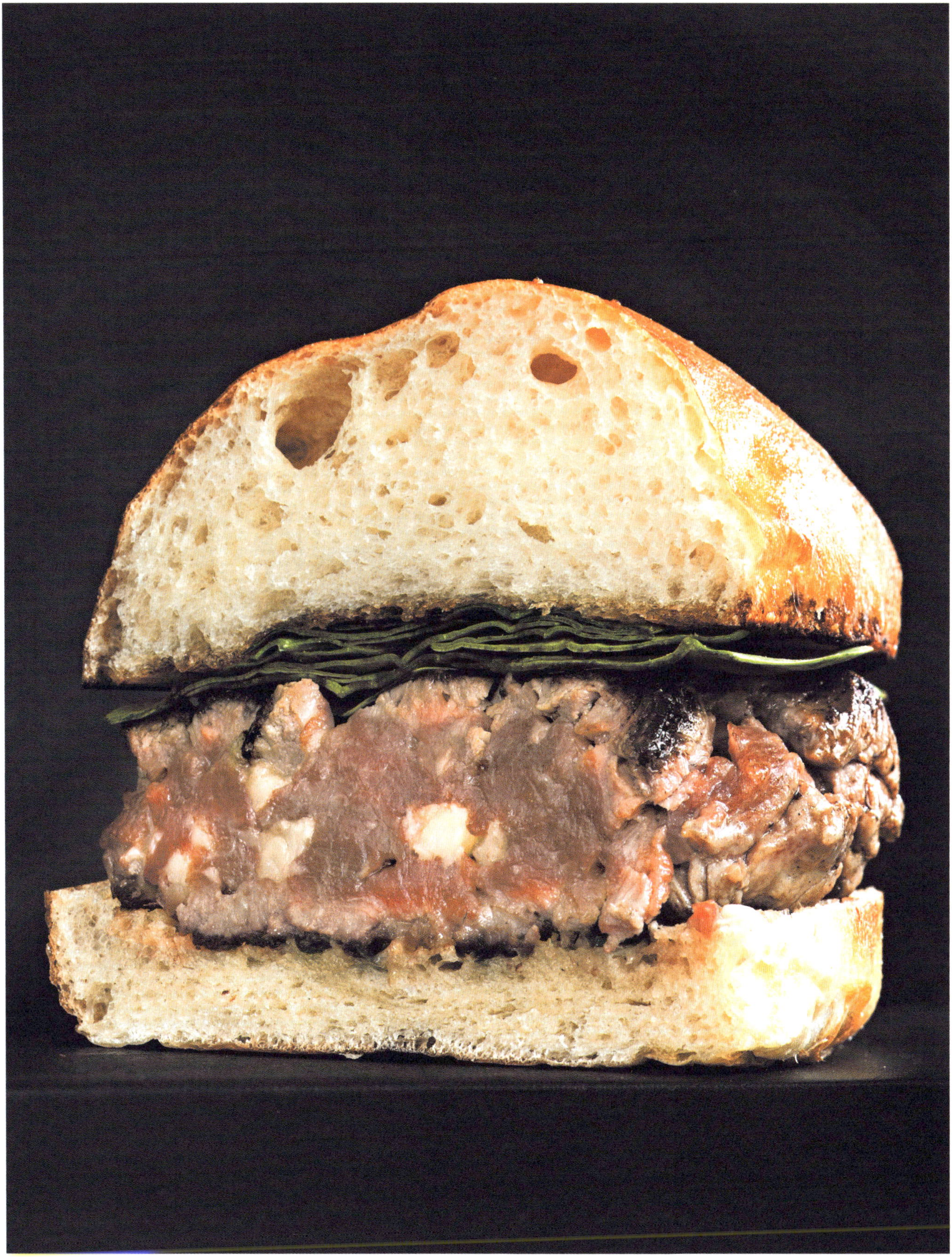

RECIPE NO. 51

MANGO

LOBSTER, MANGO

Level of difficulty:
Preparation time: 30 mins
Number of hamburgers: 4

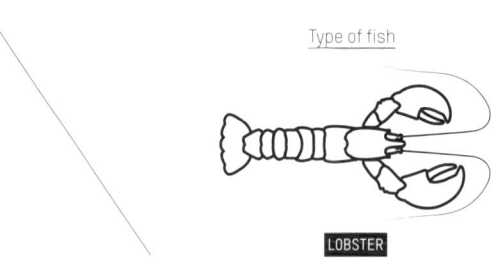

Type of fish

LOBSTER

BUNS
homemade or bought buns 4

PATTIES
lobster tails, shelled .... **500 g (1 lb 2 oz)**
butter .... **1 knob**

RELISH
mangoes, finely diced **2**
vegetable oil .... **1 teaspoon**
flat-leaf (Italian) parsley, chopped
.... **5 leaves**

SAUCE
lime (juice) **1**
crème fraîche .... **2 tablespoons**

TOPPINGS
rocket (arugula) .... **a large handful**

BUNS
Make the buns as described on page 14 or use ready-made buns.

PATTIES
Cut the lobster into dice that are small enough to form patties. If possible, shape the patties with the help of cookie cutters so they hold together better.

RELISH
Sauté the mango in a frying pan with the vegetable oil over medium heat for 2–3 minutes. Add the parsley to the mango.

SAUCE
Combine the lime juice with the crème fraîche and add to the cooled mango relish.

COOKING THE PATTIES
Put the patties, using the cookie cutters to hold them together if necessary, in a frying pan over medium-high heat. Add the butter and cook for 3 minutes on each side.

ASSEMBLY
Cut the buns in half horizontally and toast them for 2 minutes under the grill (broiler). Spread on the cut side of the bun heels half of the mango relish, then the lobster patties, the remaining relish and a few rocket leaves. Top with the crowns.

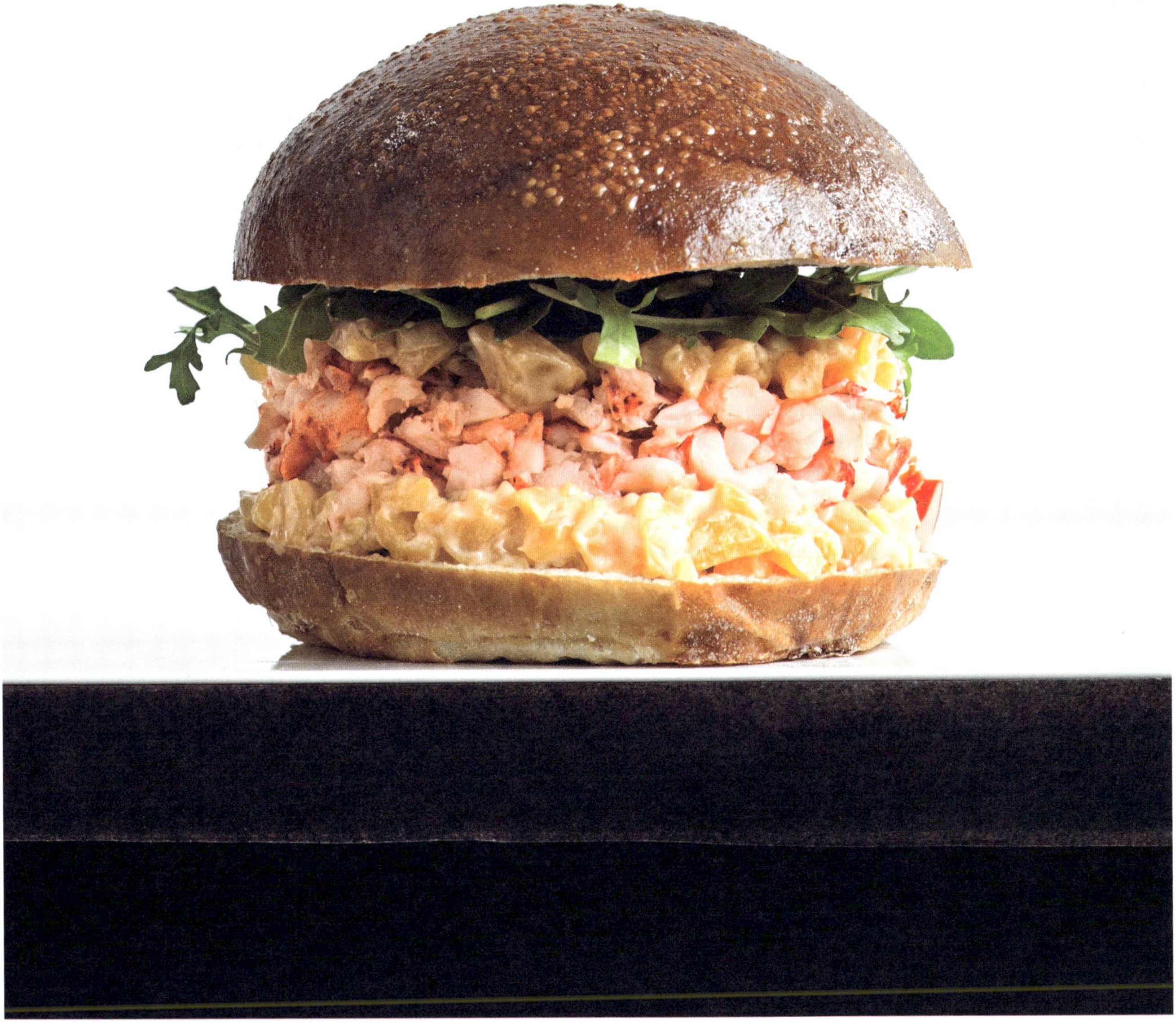

RECIPE NO. 52

JACK
SCALLOPS, COCOA

Level of difficulty: ●●
Preparation time: 25 mins
Number of hamburgers: 4

Type of fish

SCALLOPS

BUNS
homemade or bought buns — 4

PATTIES
scallops, roe removed — **440 g (15½ oz)**
unsweetened cocoa powder — **2 teaspoons**
olive oil — **100 ml (3½ fl oz)**

SAUCE
dill, chopped — **½ bunch**
crème fraîche — **80 g (2¾ oz)**
lemon (juice) — **½**

TOPPINGS
rocket (arugula) — **a large handful**

BUNS
Make the buns as described on page 14 or use ready-made buns.

PATTIES
Wash and pat the scallops dry, using paper towels. Dice the scallops and shape into 4 balls then form them into patties. If possible, shape the patties with the help of cookie cutters so they hold together better. In a bowl, combine the cocoa with the olive oil and let it rest.

SAUCE
Combine the dill with the crème fraîche and add the lemon juice.

COOKING THE PATTIES
Pour the cocoa olive oil into a frying pan over high heat and cook the patties, using the cookie cutters to hold them together if necessary, for 1½ minutes each side.

ASSEMBLY
Cut the buns in half horizontally and toast them for 2 minutes under the grill (broiler). Spread the cut side of the bun heels and crowns with the dill crème fraîche. Put the patties on the heels, followed by the rocket. Top with the crowns.

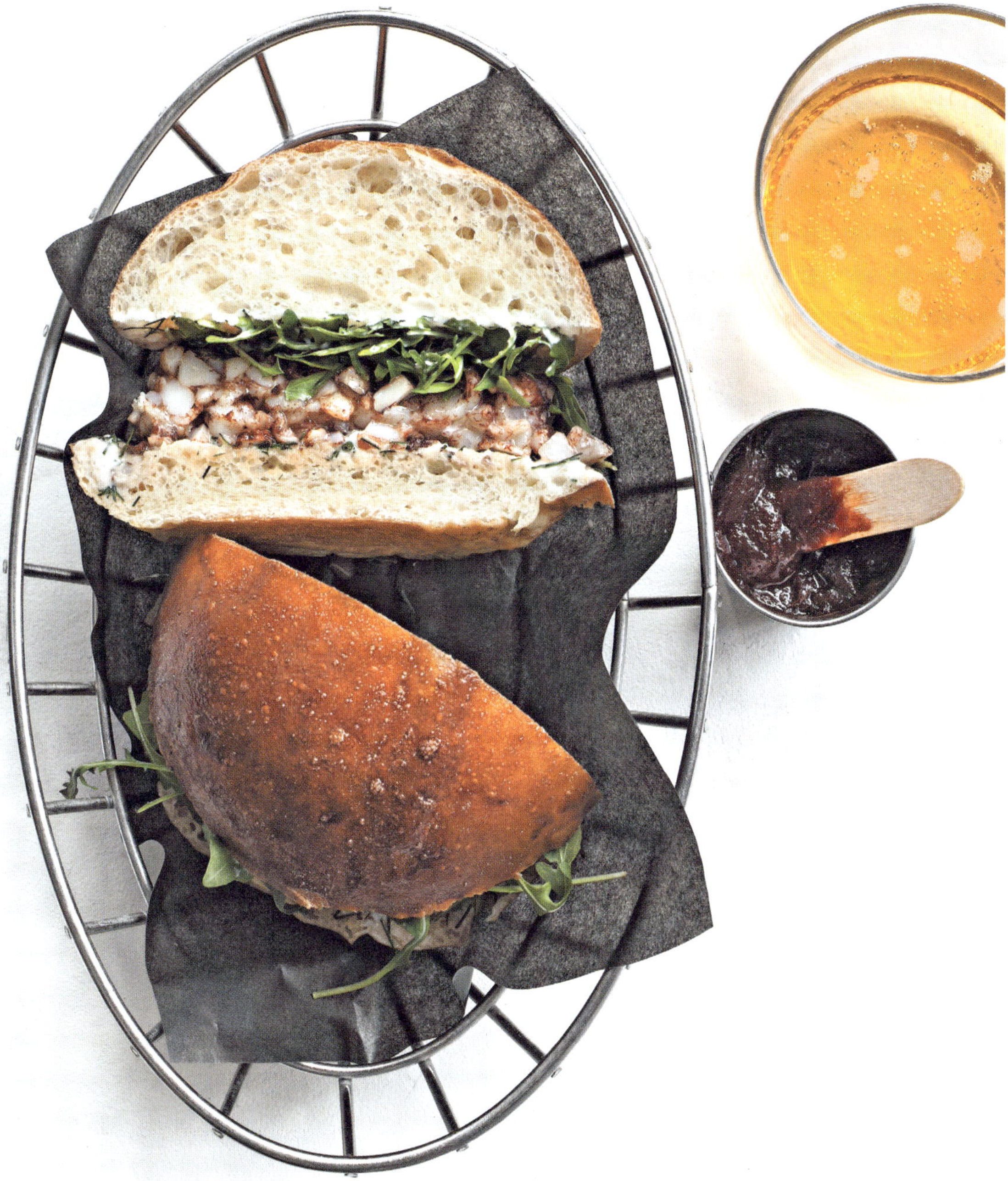

5

BLENDIES / SWEET AMERICAN TREATS WITH A FRENCH TWIST

BLENDIES

SWEET *american*

treats with

a French twist

RECIPE NO. 53

CUPCAKE
CHOCOLATE-HAZELNUT

Level of difficulty:
Preparation time: 45 mins
Number of cupcakes: 12

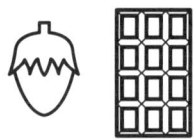

Base

HAZELNUTS + CHOCOLATE

CAKES

icing (confectioners') sugar	**200 g (7 oz)**
unsweetened cocoa powder	**1 tablespoon**
hazelnut meal	**200 g (7 oz)**
fine sea salt	**1 pinch**
egg whites	**6**
unsalted butter, melted	**200 g (7 oz)**

ICING (FROSTING)

Nutella®	**300 g (10½ oz/1¼ cups)**
unsalted butter, softened	**100 g (3½ oz)**
icing (confectioners') sugar	**50 g (1¾ oz)**
fine sea salt	**1 pinch**
crème fraîche	**1 tablespoon**
toasted hazelnuts, roughly chopped	**40 g (1½ oz/⅓ cup)**

CAKES

Preheat the oven to 200°C (400°F/Gas 6). Line a 12-hole muffin tin with paper cases or squares of baking paper folded to fit into the holes of the tin. Sift the icing sugar and cocoa powder together. Using a whisk, stir in the hazelnut meal and salt. In a large mixing bowl, whisk the egg whites until they are foamy. Add the combined dry ingredients. When the batter is smooth, add the melted butter (it should not be too hot) and mix again. Divide the batter between the holes of the muffin tin and bake for 20–25 minutes, or until firm to the touch.

ICING (FROSTING)

In a bowl, beat together the Nutella®, butter, icing sugar, salt and crème fraîche until the texture is creamy. Set aside in the refrigerator. Allow the cupcakes to cool before spreading the icing on top. To ice the cupcakes you can use a spatula, spoon or piping (icing) bag. Scatter with the toasted hazelnuts.

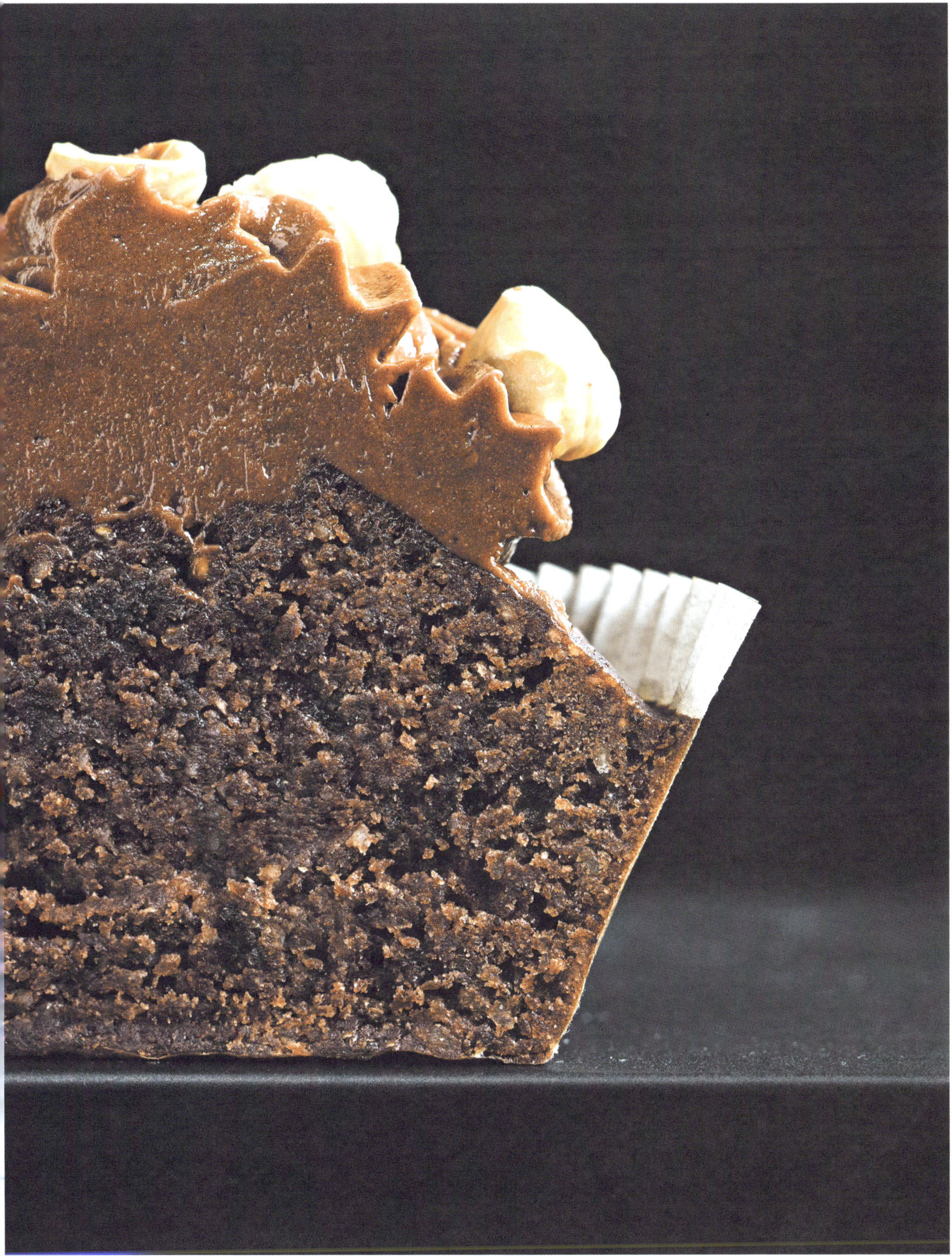

RECIPE NO. 54

BLONDIE
HAZELNUT

Level of difficulty:
Preparation time: 45 mins
Number of blondies: 12 to 16

Base

HAZELNUTS + CHOCOLATE

unsalted butter	**85 g (3 oz)**
plain (all-purpose) flour	**110 g (3¾ oz/¾ cup)**
baking powder	**½ teaspoon**
fine sea salt	**½ teaspoon**
dark brown sugar	**150 g (5½ oz/¾ cup)**
egg, beaten	**1**
natural vanilla extract	**2 teaspoons**
hazelnuts, toasted	**60 g (2¼ oz/½ cup)**
dark chocolate, coarsely chopped	**85 g (3 oz)**

PREPARATION

Make a beurre noisette: heat the butter in a saucepan over medium heat until it just begins to brown on the bottom. Pour into a bowl and allow to cool. Preheat the oven to 170°C (325°F/Gas 3). Line a 20 x 20 cm (8 x 8 inch) ceramic dish with foil and butter the foil. In a bowl, combine the flour, baking powder and salt. In a large bowl, mix together the melted butter with the sugar. Add the egg and vanilla and mix to combine. Gently fold in the flour mixture, then the hazelnuts and chocolate.

BAKING

Spoon the batter into the dish and bake for 25-30 minutes. The top should be golden and slightly cracked. Allow to cool before removing from the dish. Cut into squares to serve.

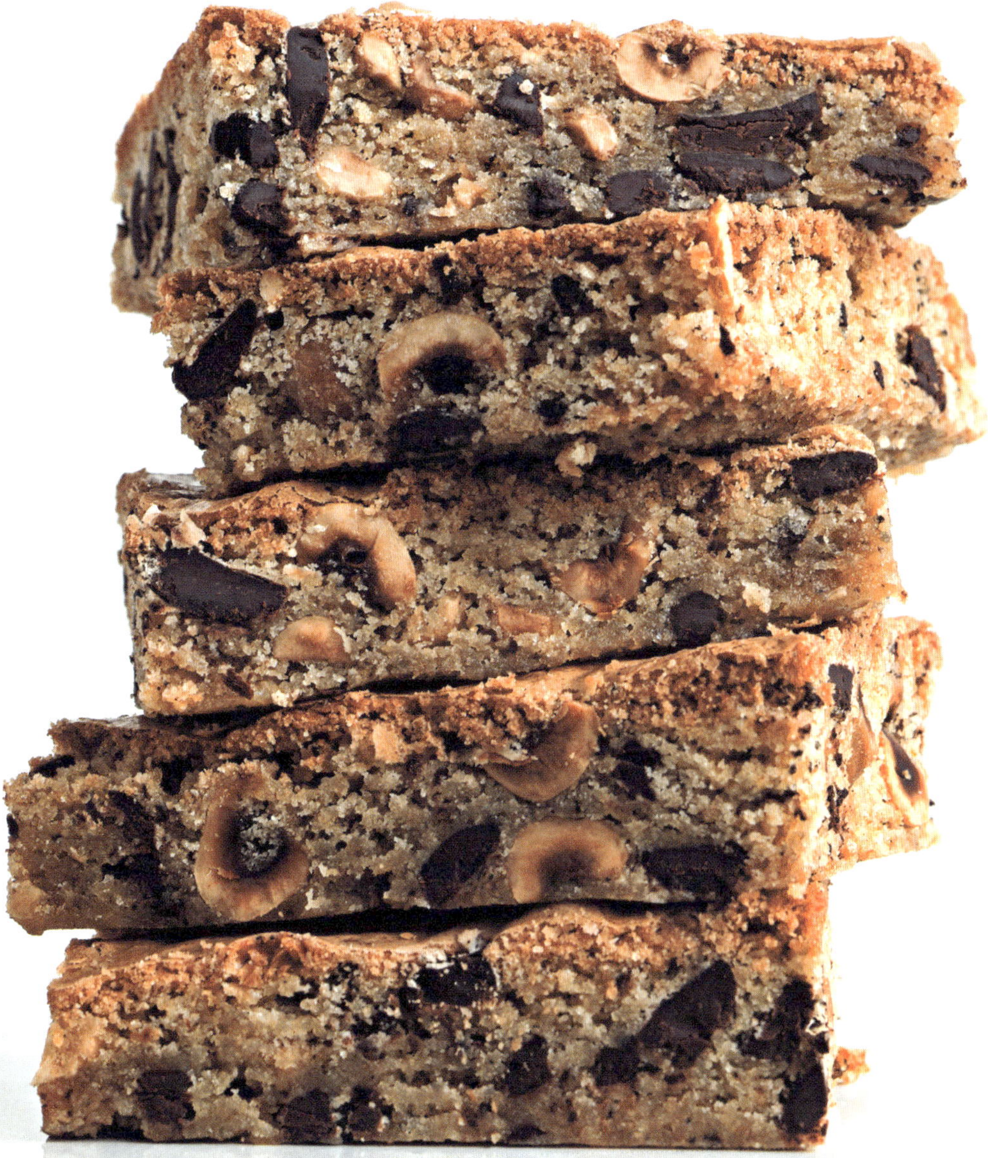

RECIPE NO. 55

WHOOPIE
CHOCOLATE, PEANUT BUTTER

Level of difficulty: 🧁🧁
Preparation time: 45 mins
Number of whoopie pies: 12

Base

PEANUTS + CHOCOLATE

CAKES

plain (all-purpose) flour	250 g (9 oz/1 ⅔ cup)
unsweetened cocoa powder	60 g (2¼ oz)
bicarbonate of soda (baking soda)	1 heaped teaspoon
fine sea salt	1 teaspoon
unsalted butter, softened	115 g (4 oz)
dark brown sugar	225 g (8 oz)
egg	1
natural vanilla extract	1 teaspoon
buttermilk	235 ml (8 fl oz)

FILLING

smooth peanut butter	200 g (7 oz)
unsalted butter, softened	100 g (3½ oz)
icing (confectioners') sugar	130 g (4½ oz)

PREPARATION

Preheat the oven to 180°C (350°F/Gas 4). Sift together the flour, cocoa powder, bicarbonate of soda and salt. Beat the butter and sugar until the mixture becomes pale. Add the egg and vanilla and beat again. Gently, add one-third of the flour mixture, then half the buttermilk, then half the remaining flour, the rest of the buttermilk and, finally, the rest of the flour.

BAKING

Drop 24 tablespoons of batter onto two baking trays lined with baking paper, spaced well apart (3–4 cm/1¼–1½ inches). Bake for about 13–15 minutes, until the cakes have puffed up and spring back when pressed. Allow to cool completely before filling.

FILLING

Beat together the peanut butter, butter and icing sugar until the texture is creamy. When the cakes have cooled, use a spoon or a piping (icing) bag to spread the peanut butter cream on half of the small cakes. Put the remaining cakes on top and press gently to stick them together.

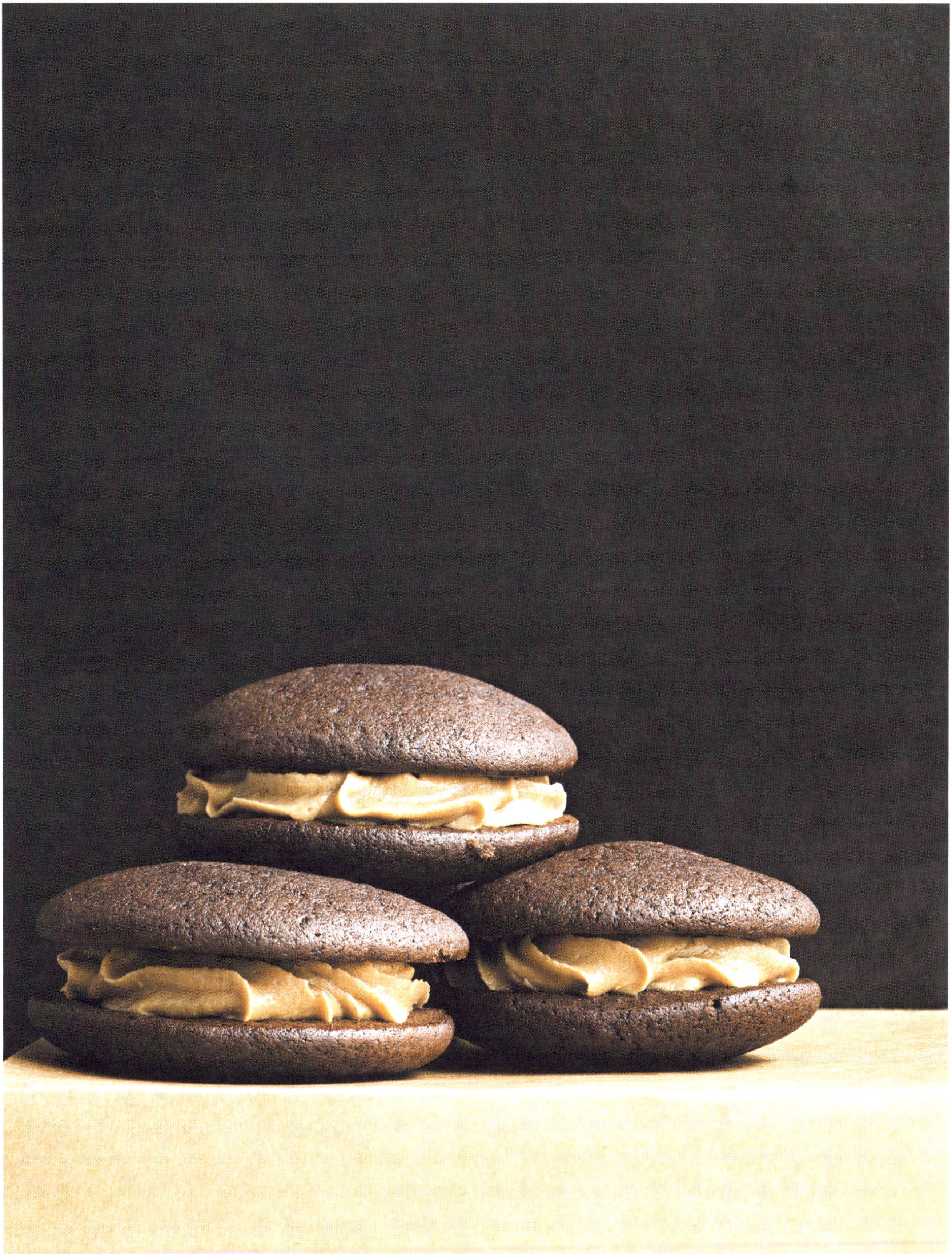

RECIPE NO. 56

M&M'S
COOKIES WITH M&M'S®

Level of difficulty:
Preparation time: 30 mins
Number of cookies: 15

Base

M&M'S

unsalted butter, softened	**70 g (2½ oz)**
dark brown sugar	**85 g (3 oz)**
caster (superfine) sugar	**45 g (1¾ oz)**
fine sea salt	**1 pinch**
egg	**1**
natural vanilla extract	**1 teaspoon**
plain (all-purpose) flour	**140 g (5 oz)**
bicarbonate of soda (baking soda)	**1 pinch**
M&M'S®	**140 g (5 oz)**

PREPARATION

Preheat the oven to 170°C (325°F/Gas 3). Beat the butter with both sugars and the salt. Add the egg and vanilla and beat again until combined. Add the flour and bicarbonate of soda and combine. When the batter is smooth, add the M&M'S® and mix again.

BAKING

On a baking tray lined with baking paper, make small mounds of batter using a tablespoon. Bake for about 12–15 minutes, until the biscuits are lightly browned around the edges.

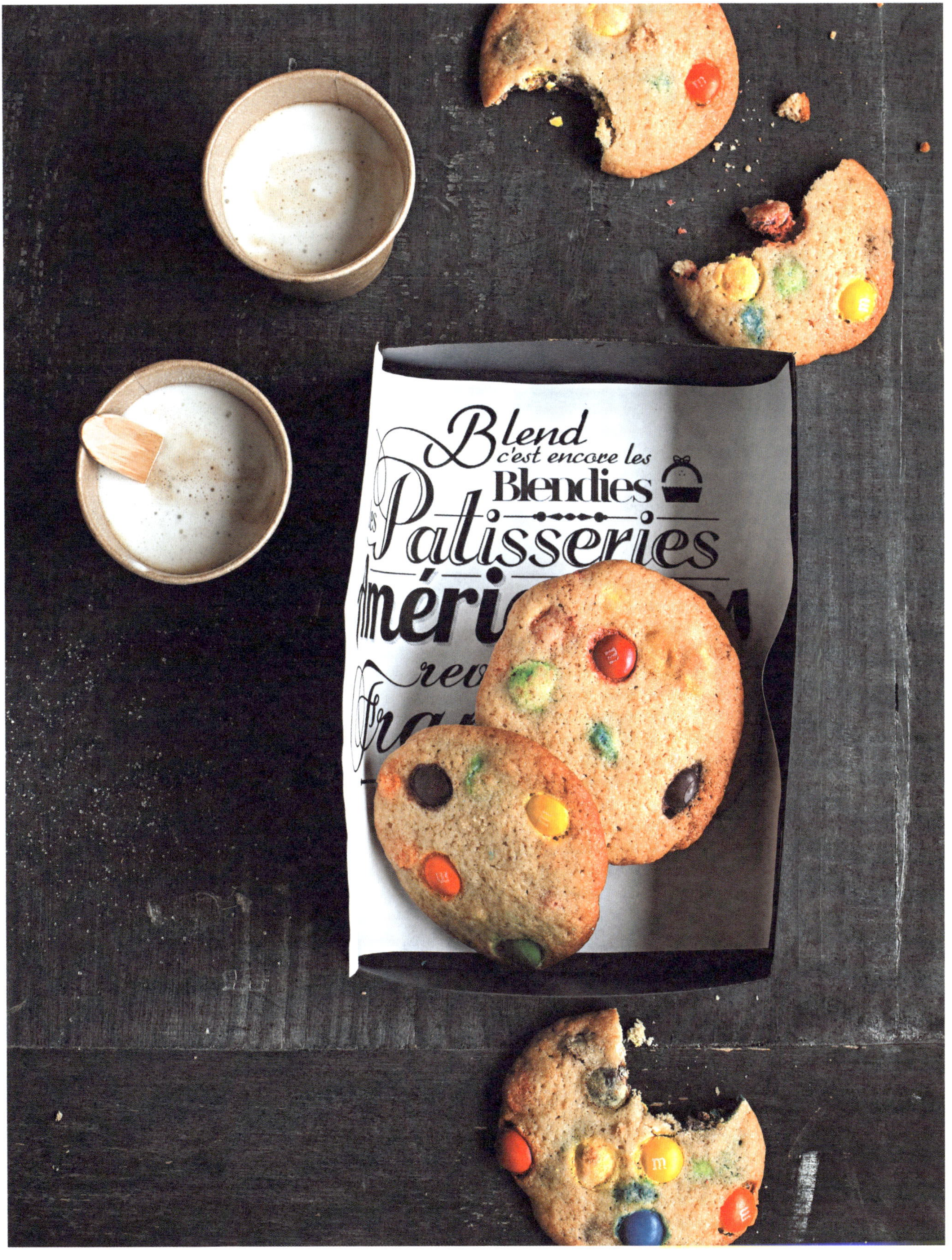
Blend
c'est encore les
Blendies
Patisseries

RECIPE NO. 57

CHEESE
CHEESECAKE

Level of difficulty: 🧁🧁🧁
Preparation time: 2 hours 15 mins + cooling and resting time
Number of serves: 8

Base

CREAM CHEESE

BASE

speculaas biscuits	100 g (3½ oz)
butter, melted	35 g (1¼ oz)
caster (superfine) sugar	1 tablespoon
fine sea salt	1 pinch

FILLING

plain cream cheese	680 g (1 lb 8 oz)
caster (superfine) sugar	180 g (6½ oz)
fine sea salt	1 pinch
eggs	3
egg yolk	1
crème fraîche	275 g (9¾ oz)
organic lemon (zest and juice)	1

BASE

Preheat the oven to 180°C (350°F/Gas 4). Crush the biscuits into fine crumbs (put them inside a freezer bag to prevent the crumbs escaping), then put them in a bowl. Add the melted butter, sugar and salt. If the mixture doesn't come together, add a few drops of water. The preparation should have a sandy texture, but hold together when pressed lightly. Pour this mixture into a 20 cm (8 inch) springform cake tin, and spread evenly over the bottom. Press down lightly with your fingers. Bake for 12 minutes, until the base is dark and grainy. Allow to cool.

FILLING

Mix the cream cheese with the sugar and salt. Add the eggs and the egg yolks, one at a time, beating well after each addition. Incorporate the crème fraîche, then the lemon zest and juice.

BAKING

Wrap the outside of the cake tin in two layers of foil. Pour the filling inside. Put the prepared tin in a wider baking dish. Pour very hot water into the dish to come halfway up the side of the cake tin. Bake at 170°C (325°F/Gas 3) for 45 minutes, then turn off the oven and leave the cheesecake in the turned-off oven for a further 1 hour. Remove the tin from the baking dish, remove the foil and allow to cool completely. If necessary, run the blade of a knife around the cheesecake to loosen before unmoulding. To serve, cut the cake into slices using a hot, dry knife. Enjoy plain or with fresh fruit (strawberries, raspberries, blueberries, blackberries, kiwi fruit, passionfruit ...) or a berry coulis.

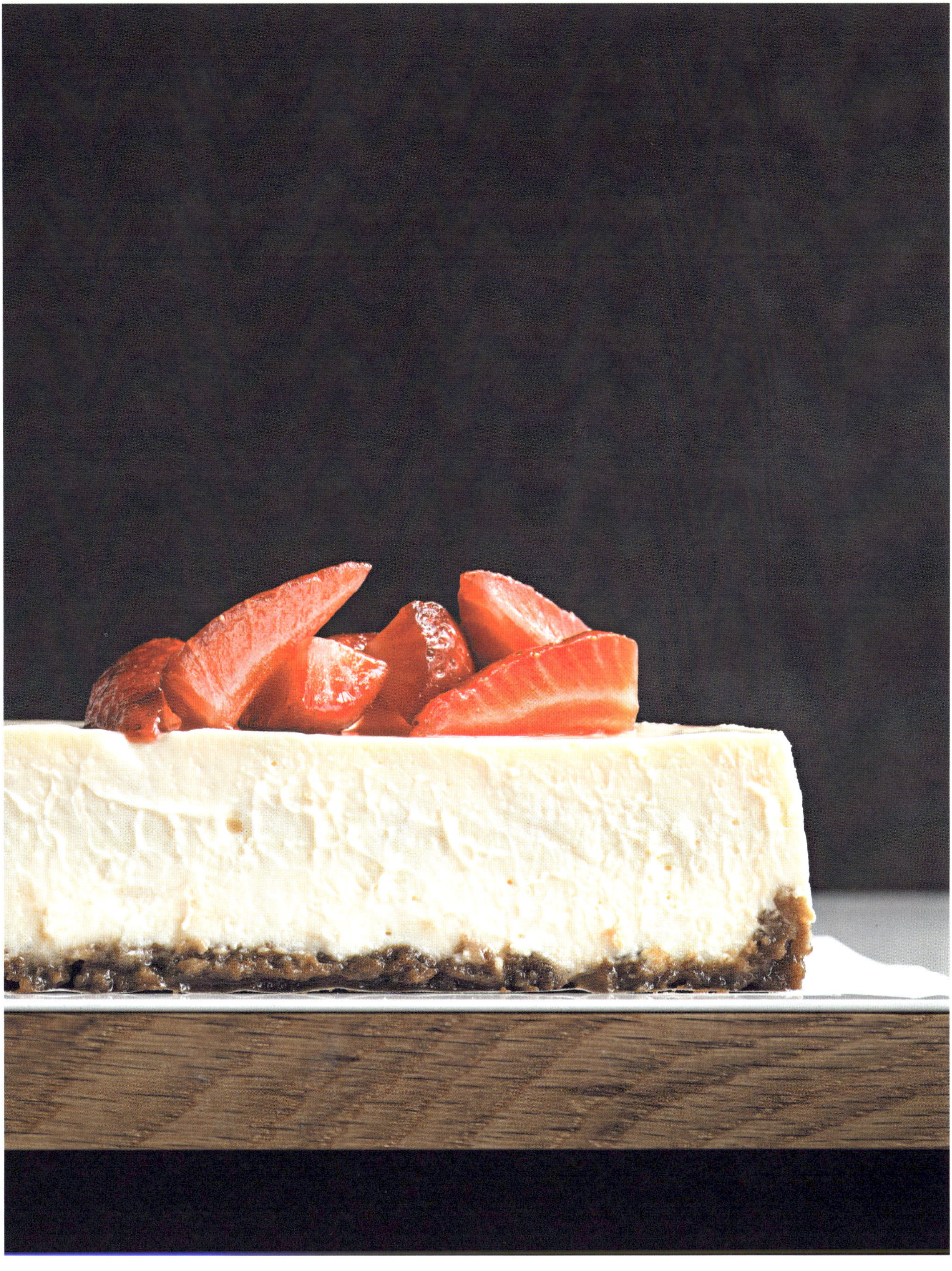

RECIPE NO. 58

UPSIDE
PINEAPPLE UPSIDE-DOWN CAKE

Level of difficulty: ●●●
Preparation time: 2 hours
Number of serves: 6–8

Base

PINEAPPLE

CARAMELISED PINEAPPLE

pineapple	1
unsalted butter	45 g (1¾ oz)
raw (demerara) sugar	200 g (7 oz)

BATTER

plain (all-purpose) flour	225 g (8 oz/1½ cups)
bicarbonate of soda (baking soda)	½ teaspoon
unsalted butter, softened	115 g (4 oz)
caster (superfine) sugar	115 g (4 oz)
dark brown sugar	85 g (3 oz)
fine sea salt	1 teaspoon
eggs	3
natural vanilla extract	1 teaspoon
American whisky	1 tablespoon
plain yoghurt	125 g (4½ oz)

CARAMELISED PINEAPPLE

Peel the pineapple with a sharp knife. Cut into quarters and remove the hard core. Cut into slices 5 mm (¼ inch) thick. Melt the butter with the raw sugar in a large non-stick frying pan. Add the slices of pineapple and cook for about 10 minutes, until they become soft. Drain in a sieve and collect the juice. Return the juice to the frying pan and bring to a simmer until it caramelises. When bubbles start to become large, pour this caramel into a 1.25 litre (44 fl oz/5 cup) capacity ceramic dish, about 20 x 20 cm (8 x 8 inches). Arrange the cooked pineapple slices over the caramel in the dish.

BATTER

Preheat the oven to 190°C (375°F/Gas 5). In a mixing bowl, combine the flour and the bicarbonate of soda. In another mixing bowl, beat the butter, the two sugars and the salt until the mixture becomes pale. Add the eggs, one at a time, beating well after each addition. Then add the vanilla and the whisky and beat again. Gently incorporate half the flour mixture, then the yoghurt and finish with the remaining flour. Spoon this batter over the pineapple pieces in the dish. Spread to make an even layer of batter.

BAKING

Bake for 45–50 minutes to 1 hour, until a small knife inserted into the centre of the cake comes out clean. Allow to cool for 10–15 minutes. Loosen the side from the dish using a knife, put a plate over the dish and turn them both over. Remove the dish. Serve hot or warm.

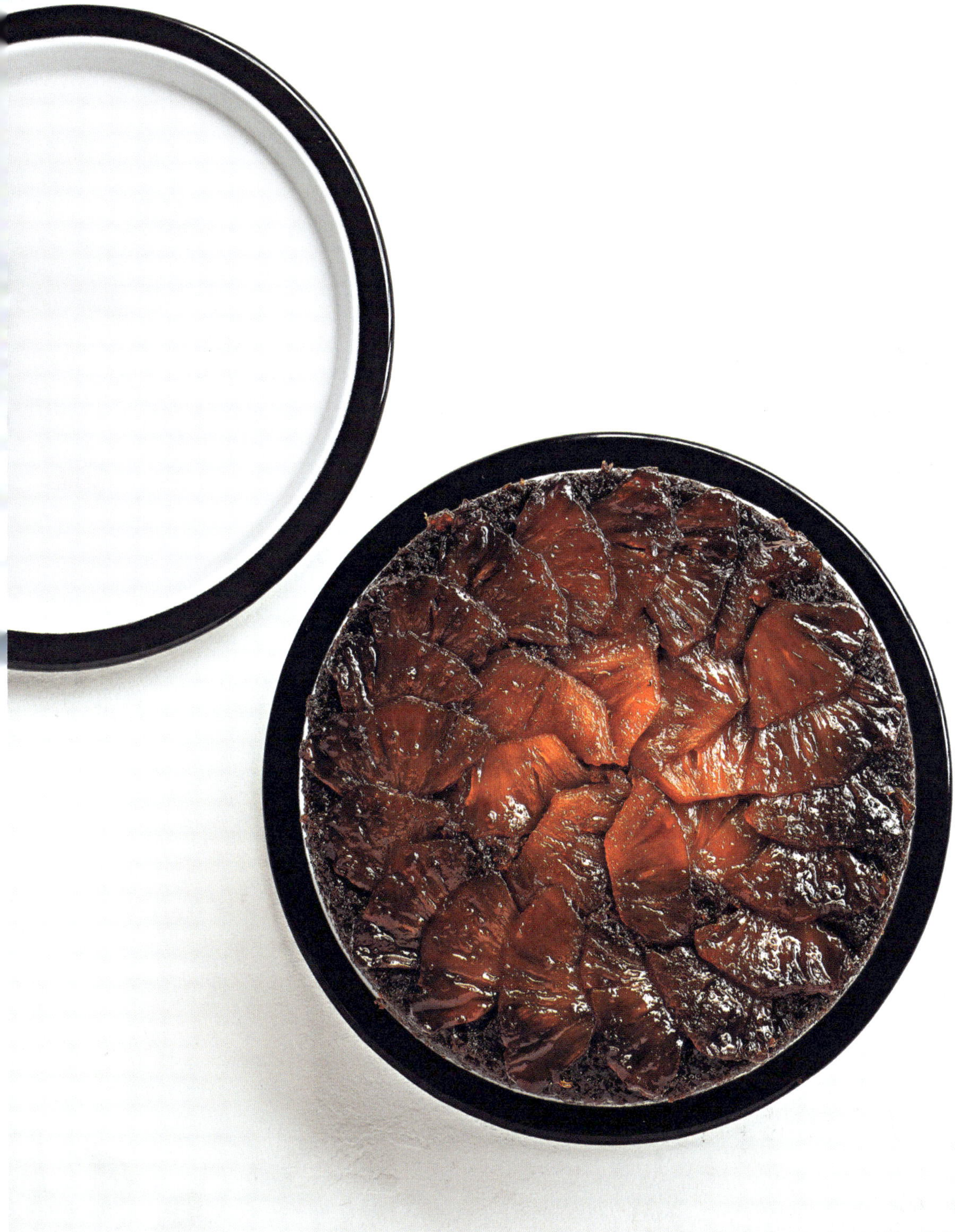

THANK YOU

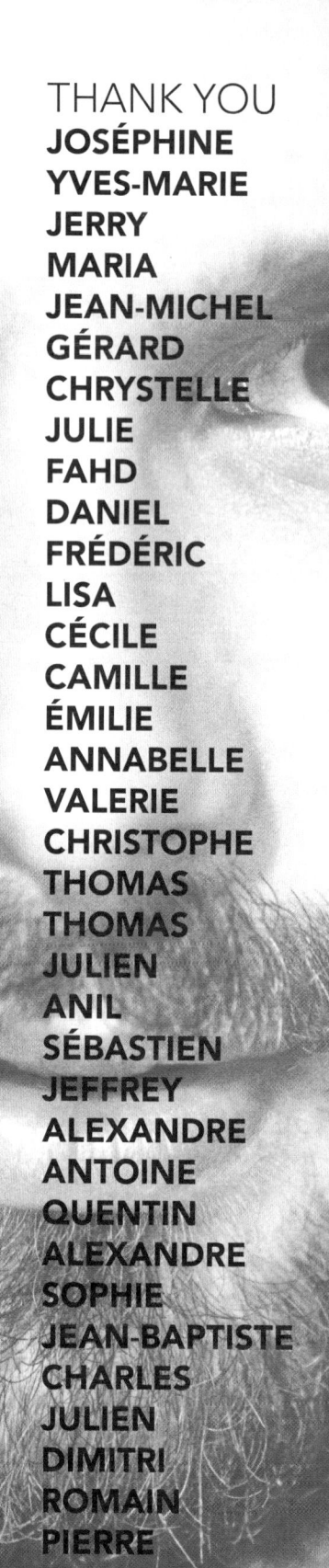

JOSÉPHINE	FABIENNE
YVES-MARIE	RALPH
JERRY	ALEXANDRA
MARIA	NATHALIE
JEAN-MICHEL	JACKIE
GÉRARD	HUBERT
CHRYSTELLE	SACHA
JULIE	SIMON
FAHD	PHILIPPE
DANIEL	NATASHA
FRÉDÉRIC	LUDIVINE
LISA	MICHAEL
CÉCILE	NICOLAS
CAMILLE	ADRIEN
ÉMILIE	VALENTIN
ANNABELLE	CLARISSE
VALERIE	ALBANE
CHRISTOPHE	ROSE
THOMAS	DOUG
THOMAS	JULIEN
JULIEN	ARNAUD
ANIL	SYLVAIN
SÉBASTIEN	MEDHI
JEFFREY	PHILIPPE
ALEXANDRE	DANY
ANTOINE	JULIEN
QUENTIN	BERTRAND
ALEXANDRE	CLÉMENT
SOPHIE	AYMERIC
JEAN-BAPTISTE	GUY PAUL
CHARLES	COLIN
JULIEN	JEANINE
DIMITRI	VALHÉRY
ROMAIN	DIDIER
PIERRE	ANGELO
	PIERRE-ÉDOUARD

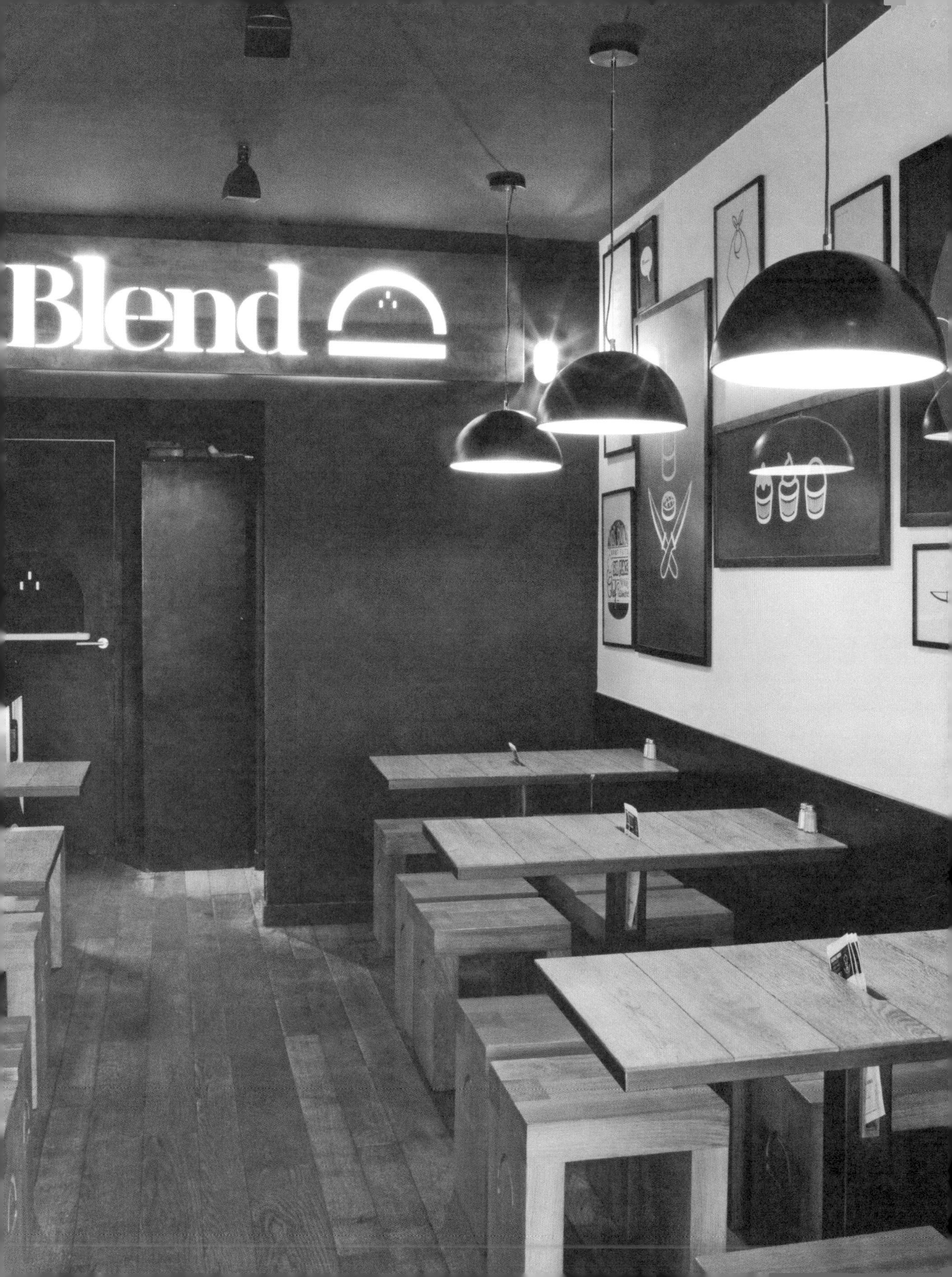
Blend

INDEX OF RECIPES

DISSECTION
bun	14
onion relish	22
apple-shallot relish	22
parsnip-spring onion relish	22
barbecue	26
chipotle	26
ketchup	26
garlic mayonnaise	26
chips	28

PURE
base	32
bake	34
brie	36
feta	38
mozza	40
cherry	42
Cantal	44
mush	46
lardo	48
simple	50
sun	52
wine	54
beet	56
chick	58
basque	60
coco	62
red	64
quince	66
herbs	68
sweet	70
funghi	72
magret	74
fish	76
salmon	78
spicy	80
thai	82
cod	84
ace	86
radish	88

MIX
blue	92
scotch	94
ring	96
beer	98
diablo	100
pesto	102
chorizo	104
honey	106
ross	108
milk	110
taj	112
mex	114
bbq	116
creo	118

VEGGIE
quinoa	122
greenie	124
beans	126
burg	128
tofu	130
chill	132

RECIPES FROM THE CHEF
meat	136
mango	138
jack	140

BLENDIES
cupcake	144
blondy	146
whoop	148
M&M'S	150
cheese	152
upside	154

INDEX BY INGREDIENT

AVOCADO
mex	114

BACON
bake	34
diablo	100

BEANS
beans	126
burg	128
chill	132
greenie	124

BEEF
bake	34
base	32
beer	98
beet	56
blue	92
brie	36
Cantal	44
cherry	42
chorizo	104
diablo	100
feta	38
honey	106
lardo	48
meat	136
mozza	40
mush	46
pesto	102
ring	96
ross	108
scotch	94
simple	50
sun	52
wine	54

BEETROOT
beet	56
quinoa	122
red	64

BLACK RADISH
radish	88

BLEU D'AUVERGNE
blue	92

BRIE
brie	36

BURGHUL (BULGUR)
burg	128
quinoa	122

CAPSICUM (PEPPER)
basque	60
scotch	94
spicy	80
sweet	70

CANTAL
Cantal	44

CARROT
Cantal	44
greenie	124
herbs	68
radish	88
sweet	70

CHEDDAR
bake	34
diablo	100
scotch	94

CHEESE, SHEEP'S MILK
beer	98
cherry	42

CHICKEN
basque	60
chick	58
coco	62
quince	66
mex	114
red	64

CHOCOLATE
blondy	146

CHORIZO
chorizo	104

CRAB
creo	118

CREAM CHEESE
cheese	152

COCONUT CREAM
coco	62

COCOA
cupcake	144
jack	140
whoop	148

COD
cod	84
fish	76

CORN
chill 132

DUCK
magret 74

EGGPLANT (AUBERGINE)
sun 52

FENNEL
simple 50

FETA
feta 38

FIG
Cantal 44

FOIE GRAS
ross 108

FRENCH SHALLOT
Cantal 44
creo 118
quince 66
wine 54

GHERKIN (PICKLE)
bake 34
base 32

GINGERBREAD
ross 108

GOAT CHEESE
sun 52

GORGONZOLA
quince 66
pesto 102

GOUDA
mex 114

GRAPE
Cantal 44
taj 112

GRUYÈRE
funghi 72

HAZELNUT
blondy 146
cupcake 144

LAMB
herbs 68
milk 110
taj 112

LARDO DI COLONNATA
lardo 48

LENTILS
beans 126

LOBSTER
mango 138

M&M'S
M&M'S 150

MANGO
mango 138

MOZZARELLA
mozza 40

MUSHROOM
mush 46
funghi 72

ONION
base 32
basque 60
beer 98
brie 36
chorizo 104
coco 62
ring 96
ross 108
simple 50
spicy 80

PARMESAN
pesto 102
sweet 70

PINEAPPLE
ace 86
upside 154

POTATO
greenie 124
magret 74

PORK
ace 86
bbq 116
radish 88

PRAWN
thai 82

PRUNE
taj 112

QUINCE
quince 66

QUINOA
quinoa 122

RED WINE
wine 54

SALMON
salmon 78

SCALLOPS
jack 140

TOFU
tofu 130

TOMATO
bake 34
basque 60
chorizo 104
feta 38
simple 50
spicy 80
sun 52

TUNA
spicy 80

VEAL
funghi 72
sweet 70

ZUCCHINI (COURGETTE)
greenie 124
tofu 130

THIS EDITION PUBLISHED IN 2017 BY MURDOCH BOOKS, AN IMPRINT OF ALLEN & UNWIN.
FIRST PUBLISHED BY MARABOUT IN 2012.
PUBLISHED IN 2013 BY MURDOCH BOOKS.

MURDOCH BOOKS AUSTRALIA
83 ALEXANDER STREET
CROWS NEST NSW 2065
PHONE: +61 (0) 2 8425 0100
FAX: +61 (0) 2 9906 2218
WWW.MURDOCHBOOKS.COM.AU
INFO@MURDOCHBOOKS.COM.AU

MURDOCH BOOKS UK
ORMOND HOUSE
26-27 BOSWELL STREET
LONDON WC1N 3JZ
PHONE: +44 (0) 20 7269 1610
WWW.MURDOCHBOOKS.CO.UK
INFO@MURDOCHBOOKS.CO.UK

FOR CORPORATE ORDERS & CUSTOM PUBLISHING CONTACT NOEL HAMMOND,
NATIONAL BUSINESS DEVELOPMENT MANAGER, MURDOCH BOOKS AUSTRALIA

PUBLISHER: CORINNE ROBERTS
PHOTOGRAPHER: DAVID JAPY
STYLIST: ELODIE RAMBAUD
PASTRY RECIPES: CAMILLE MALMQUIST
GRAPHIC DESIGN AND ILLUSTRATIONS: MINSK-STUDIO
TRANSLATOR: MELISSA MCMAHON
EDITOR: SOPHIA ORAVECZ
FOOD EDITOR: CHRISTINE OSMOND
RECIPE TESTING: GRACE CAMPBELL
PROJECT EDITOR: HENRIETTA ASHTON
PRODUCTION: RACHEL WALSH

TEXT AND DESIGN © HACHETTE LIVRE (MARABOUT) 2012

ALL RIGHTS RESERVED. NO PART OF THIS PUBLICATION MAY BE REPRODUCED, STORED IN A RETRIEVAL SYSTEM OR TRANSMITTED IN ANY FORM OR BY ANY MEANS, ELECTRONIC, MECHANICAL, PHOTOCOPYING, RECORDING OR OTHERWISE, WITHOUT THE PRIOR WRITTEN PERMISSION OF THE PUBLISHER.

A CATALOGUING-IN-PUBLICATION ENTRY IS AVAILABLE FROM THE CATALOGUE OF THE NATIONAL LIBRARY OF AUSTRALIA AT WWW.NLA.GOV.AU.

A CATALOGUE RECORD FOR THIS BOOK IS AVAILABLE FROM THE BRITISH LIBRARY.

ISBN 978 1 76052 259 9 AUSTRALIA
ISBN 978 1 76052 266 7 UK

COLOUR REPRODUCTION BY SPLITTING IMAGE, CLAYTON, VICTORIA.
PRINTED BY 1010 PRINTING.

IMPORTANT: THOSE WHO MIGHT BE AT RISK FROM THE EFFECTS OF SALMONELLA POISONING (THE ELDERLY, PREGNANT WOMEN, YOUNG CHILDREN AND THOSE SUFFERING FROM IMMUNE DEFICIENCY DISEASES) SHOULD CONSULT THEIR DOCTOR WITH ANY CONCERNS ABOUT EATING RAW EGGS.

OVEN GUIDE: YOU MAY FIND COOKING TIMES VARY DEPENDING ON THE OVEN YOU ARE USING. FOR FAN-FORCED OVENS, AS A GENERAL RULE, SET THE OVEN TEMPERATURE TO 20°C (70°F) LOWER THAN INDICATED IN THE RECIPE.

MEASURES GUIDE: WE HAVE USED 20 ML (4 TEASPOON) TABLESPOON MEASURES. IF YOU ARE USING A 15 ML (3 TEASPOON) TABLESPOON ADD AN EXTRA TEASPOON OF THE INGREDIENT FOR EACH TABLESPOON SPECIFIED.

THE STYLIST WOULD LIKE TO THANK THE FOLLOWING SUPPLIERS:
HABITAT: WWW.HABITAT.FR
CONRAN SHOP: WWW.CONRANSHOP.FR
MUJI: WWW.MUJI.FR

TEXAS 1880 / NYC 1885

1916 $ TEXAS

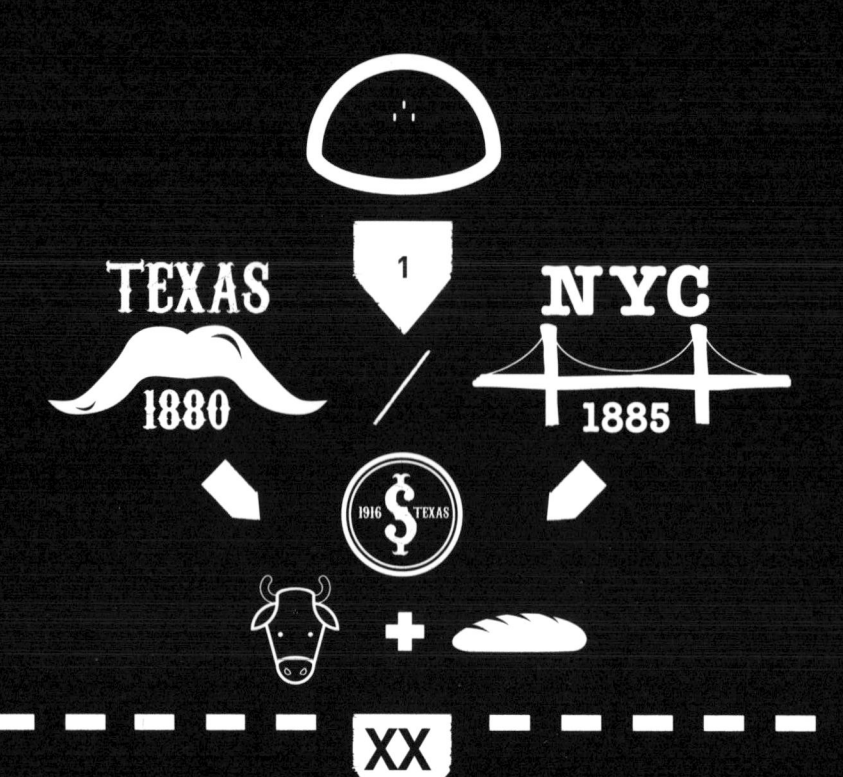

🐄 + 🥖

40s
KANSAS · BIG BOY
WHITE CASTLE · MC DONALD'S

2000
Daniel Boulud

Gourmet Hamburger

TRADITIONAL HAMBURGER